simply elegant flowers

WITH MICHAEL GEORGE

simply elegant flowers

WITH MICHAEL GEORGE

WRITTEN WITH BOB SHUMAN
FOREWORD BY MARTHA STEWART

NORTH LIGHT BOOKS

CINCINNATI, OHIO

Simply Elegant Flowers with Michael George Copyright © 2008 by Michael George. Manufactured in China. All rights reserved. It is permissible for the purchaser to make the projects contained herein and sell them at fairs, bazaars and craft shows. No other part of this book may be reproduced in any form or by any electronic or mechanical means including information storage and retrieval systems without permission in writing from the publisher, except by a reviewer, who may quote a brief passage in review. Published by North Light Books, an imprint of F+W Publications, Inc., 4700 East Galbraith Road, Cincinnati, Ohio 45236. (800) 289-0963. First edition.

12 11 10 09 08   5 4 3 2 1

Library of Congress Cataloging-in-Publication Data

George, Michael, 1947-
  Simply elegant flowers with Michael George / Michael George written with Bob Shuman.
      p. cm.
  Includes index.
  ISBN 978-1-55870-806-8
  1. Flower arrangement. I. Shuman, Bob. II. Title.

SB449.G46 2007
745.92--dc22
                              2007031569

Distributed in Canada by Fraser Direct
100 Armstrong Avenue
Georgetown, ON, Canada L7G 5S4
Tel: (905) 877-4411

Distributed in the U.K. and Europe by David & Charles
Brunel House, Newton Abbot, Devon, TQ12 4PU, England
Tel: (+44) 1626 323200, Fax: (+44) 1626 323319
E-mail: postmaster@davidandcharles.co.uk

Distributed in Australia by Capricorn Link
P.O. Box 704, South Windsor, NSW 2756 Australia
Tel: (02) 4577-3555

editor: Jessica Strawser
cover photographer: Brie Williams
project coordinator/stylist: Lisa George
cover designer: Amanda Dalton
interior designer: Karla Baker
interior layout & production: Kelly O'Dell
production coordinator: Greg Nock

fw
F+W PUBLICATIONS, INC.
www.fwpublications.com

PHOTO BY BRIE WILLIAMS

ADDITIONAL PHOTOGRAPHY

Pages 2 and 3: Roses by Brie Williams. Page 94: Clematis by Gino Santa; Daffodil by Ayesa Wilson. Page 98: Peony by Carole Gomez; Sweet Pea by Tamara Kulikova. Page 99: Cherry Branch by Marek Cech; Pear Branch by Narcisa Buzxlea; Forsythia Branch by Mary Morgan. Page 111: Carnation by Gina Luck; Sunflower by Bruce Bean. Page 122: Heliconia by Timur Kulgarin; Bird of Paradise by David Schrader. Page 124: Agapanthus by Karin Lau; Allium by Carole Gomez. Page 125: Cat tail Foliage by Heiko Grossman; Cornflower by Anna Khomulo; Chamomile by Jasmin Awad. Page 126: Eremurus by Stuart Brill; Dahlia by Olga Ekaterincheva; Daisy by Simon McConico; Delphenium by Tamara Kulikova. Page 127: Euphorbia by Suzanne Carter-Jackson. Page 128: Hosta by Sally Scott; Lisianthus by Oksana Struk; Monkshood by Christina Richards. Page 129: Phlox by Elena Blokhina. Page 130: Sunflowers by Bruce Bean. Page 144: Coral Sunset Peony by Gina Luck. Page 160: Amaranthus by Chartchai Messangnin; Bittersweet vines by Klaus Janssen; Celosia by Mark Hayes Photography. Page 162: Kale by Gina Luck; Maple by Tony Squeo; Pear foliage by Heather Faye Bath. Page 163: Sedum by Anneclaire Le Royer; Seedpods by Melissa Carroll; Sunflower by Jennifer Daley; Vibernum by Vladimir Konjushenko. Page 172: Spider Mum by Candice Cusack; Statesman Mums by Anna Bryukhanova; Snowdrift Mums by Cathleen Abers-Kimball. Page 174: Poinsettia by Andrzej Tokarski; Rose by Andrea Manciu; Shamrocks by Denise Bentley. Page 193: Phalaenopsis Orchid by Diane Diederich. Page 194: Baby's Breath by Susan Fox. Page 195: Gardenia by Igor Zhorov; Jasmine by Kjell Brynildsen. Page 197: Orchids by Steve Dibblee. Page 198: Quince by Klaus Janssen; Lamb's Ear by Andrew Dean; Eucalyptus by Patricia Nason.

Dedication

For my father.

PHOTO BY BRIE WILLIAMS

acknowledgments

I would like to thank Avant Garden, Karla Baker, Cynthia Black, Edgar Bout, Ming Chung, June Clark, Gardencio and Gabriel Contreras, Amanda Dalton, Christine Doyle, Tom Fagan, F+W Publications, Lisa George, Pam Green, Carl Grimes and all at Dutch Flowerline, Rob Houtenbos, Eileen Johnson, Calvin Klein, Peter Lozer, Stuart Marshall, Eve Marx, Kate McGinty, Bill Miller, Mother Nature, Nancy Nelson and Randy Lanchner, Gary Page, Oscar de la Renta, Michele Rosenbloom, Kathleen Ross, Peter Rubie, Karen Schimmel, Ian Schrager, Bob and Marit Shuman, the Shuman and Nolan families, Rita Battat Silverman and Steve Silverman, Jessica Strawser, Louis Theofaris, Saki Tornasakis, Cas Trap, Robert Treadway, Mikey and Bella Vasillopulos, Patricia Waddell, Vera Wang, Diego and Cynthia Weingartener, and Brie Williams. Thanks also, in memory, to Bill Blass, Pat Buckley and Glen Birnbaum. And a special thanks to my friend Martha Stewart.

contents

foreword

BY MARTHA STEWART

I wish you could have seen my home last evening. It was pure Michael George, or at least as close as I could come to his style and beauty without having Michael there himself. I was having a dinner party—an autumnal supper of root vegetable soup, choucroute garni and lemon curd tart—and I wanted my flowers to reflect the season, the colorful fall foliage, and the simple but restrained elegance of the rustic menu. So I arranged dozens of orange tulips exactly as I had been taught by Michael himself, with neatly stripped stems, perfectly aligned, carefully secured with a transparent rubber band (really a ponytail rubber band), the bunches gently twisted so stems and blossoms alike were vibrantly positioned in clear class containers. I put four identical vases on the dining table, one on the living room desk surrounded by amber glass turkeys, a giant bowl in the entry hall and others on side tables. When finished with the task, which I admit took a little longer than a blink of an eye, I did think of my mentor Michael and thought, "He would certainly approve."

A signature Michael George arrangement of white tulips
in a ceramic bowl
PHOTO BY BRIE WILLIAMS

9

I first noticed Michael's work in the Calvin Klein store in New York City. I was so entranced with the voluptuous, full, elegant, modern arrangements of white roses, calla lilies and ranunculus that I asked for the name of the designer. I started using Michael personally as well as professionally and invited him numerous times to teach his craft on my television show. He also made my daughter's beautiful wedding flowers, and has contributed many times to our publications.

Michael, throughout his career, has remained true to his simple and forthright philosophy. For the serious observer, like me, his insistence on the freshest ingredients, pristine flowers, impeccable preparation, precise tools, an almost surgically immaculate working environment and unusual but simply modern containers is evident in each and every arrangement he creates. And for me it is very hard to choose a favorite from Michael's approaches or designs, because the underlying tenets are strictly enforced in all of Michael's work. Whether he makes a small cylindrical bunch of grape hyacinths or a larger monotone gathering of white roses, stars of Bethlehem and hyacinths, you can be certain the result will be stunning and breathtaking.

Somehow the floral designer with two first names has always understood Albert Einstein's directive that what he does should always be simple but never, ever, too simple.

A contemporary twist on yellow miniature calla lilies in
a graphic glass bowl-shaped vase
PHOTO BY BRIE WILLIAMS

Think of the seasons in Italian: *quattro stagione*, the four stages of nature. The dazzling yet always stately passage; the anticipation, peak and finish of each time of year. In the art of flower arranging, during the procession, I note symmetries as well as the synchronized movements of blooms seeking the sun. When I actually touch them, I connect physically with these ever-changing, ever-constant stages, and I am overcome by a sense of well-being.

My mother brought me to my father's flower shop when I was three days old. Leaving New York Hospital with me, she took a bus to Eighty-sixth and First. Six months later, crawling around the floor of the store where the stems dropped, I learned smells, textures and tastes. I worked here after school as I grew older and spent Sunday mornings with my mentor, Abel Parmentola, a botanist who as a young man had designed floral displays for the Italian royal family. He was the designer behind Judith Garten and Ethel Rogers,

top New York florists from the 1940s through the 1960s. "I'm a very old man," Parmentola told me as he taught me his repertoire of hundreds of original bouquets, "so you got to keep your mouth shut and your eyes open 'cause I only show you everything one time, that's it."

Here, during the 1940s, the flower industry was being reinvented. Its previous history in America was rather dull, confined to churches, weddings, funerals and boxes. I was drawn to an arranger at the Savoy Plaza Hotel, a leader my father and his contemporaries always referred to. He was famous for a notable, low-profile bouquet: concentric, alternating carnation-and-daisy rings that culminated at streamers in the center. His black-framed shop window, an example of ultra-chic 1930s simplicity, read only: "Max Schling, Flowers." Probably my most personal influence, however, was my dad, George Christ Vasillopulos, who taught me for twenty-six years. I idolized him. As a medic stationed in postwar Tokyo, he saw the people buying flowers on the ravaged streets. His girlfriend, a practitioner of Ikebana, the Japanese art of floral arranging, began teaching him. Recognizing a need to

Posing with some freshly arranged favorites: Italian ranunculus
PHOTO BY BRIE WILLIAMS

improve the industry in the United States, he felt Americans would take flowers into their everyday lives. On his return he began selling flowers in simple vases (in fact, mostly Haeger and Roseville vases, which are now very collectable). It was an innovative concept because at the time, flowers given as gifts were packaged or boxed; only expensive custom floral designers delivered their arrangements in containers. Dad later became a charter member of FTD and conducted many commercial tests on new industry innovations, such as OASIS Floral Foam.

QUATTRO STAGIONE

It occurred to me to write a book on simple and elegant flower arranging in the real time of the *quattro stagione*. This way, using many settings, some in a studio and some in nature, I could capture some of the unlimited, everyday reasons for displaying florals at home. I felt that this was the best way to show the possibilities of assembling blooms on a daily basis, the way I live with them always nearby, and it would allow me to show you how I work in a relaxed, casual way. What many find astounding is that it's impossible to make a mistake with flowers. In my philosophy I attempt to arrange them as they are in nature, which is already perfect.

Head to the garden with me to make the best floral selection for a dinner party or just for everyday decor; we'll create a simple workspace and prepare and condition the blooms, working in a neat and organized way.

For spring, we'll watch the earth warm, hyacinths and anemones awaken and peonies unfurl.

We'll stuff pails or mason jars with lush sunflowers, dahlias and snapdragons during the summer.

In autumn, we'll check the colors of the changing foliage—always different, always offering fresh inspiration. Living with flowers is not just a visual experience; you'll find they highten all your senses. Soon you'll be rediscovering the scent of fall leaves burning as the trees go bare around them.

Setting ice-blue-and-white blossoms against dark green needles and cedars in winter, we'll again reap the sensory benefits of our endeavors as pine and fir emit their familiar winter perfumes.

DEFINING THE STYLE

Today, the graphic look—minimal, repeating, neatly aligned—is seen in virtually every contemporary decorating or lifestyle magazine. In the early 1980s, however—and especially within the floral community—it was an enormous departure from the day's trends and, actually, from those of previous decades: Flower displays were always expected to be big and diverse.

My father had been prophetic about Americans' interest in flowers. Although not to the extent found in Japan and Europe, they did take flowers home—especially during the rushes of holidays, occasions when customers would buy roses and poinsettias. They could also, by this time, easily place an order anywhere in the country and order a Mother's Day bouquet that would include virtually the same red

Clockwise: Spring hyacinths; summer field flower bouquet; winter amaryllis; autumn ranunculus, roses and fruits
PHOTOS BY BRIE WILLIAMS

15

Spring ranunculus in a black glass cylinder
PHOTO BY BRIE WILLIAMS

carnation ordered three thousand miles away. "Get Well Soon" displays were interchangeable between Salt Lake City and Chicago, as were spring bouquets and "Happy Birthday" arrangements relying on local floral palette variations. These could include chrysanthemum, statice, carnation, dahlia, zinnia and other seasonal crops, as well as limited varieties of exotic blooms: rose, anthurium and bird of paradise. To be honest, I always tore away the bows, ribbons and ornamentations that went with these effects, which were typically used to hide brusque work and poorer-quality flowers.

I wanted to bring florals even further into American culture, extending my father's vision. Deeply influenced by the fashion industry, I would see a design concept and begin interpreting the look through the forms and colors of flowers. (Likewise, music and other forms of art and nature did—and still do—inspire me.) I spent hours walking up and down Madison Avenue studying the store windows, paying special attention to the graphic, bold work of Bill Blass, Armani, Halston, Calvin Klein, Helmut Lang, Karl Lagerfeld and Tommy Hilfiger, to name a few. At night, I'd examine art books and *Architectural Digest*. The modern look was becoming simpler; it was reaching the everyday consumer with monochromatic T-shirts and pants from the likes of J.Crew and Gap. The design was straightforward, using good-quality natural fiber. I wanted to utilize similar concepts

in my florals. My workspace was radically minimalized, made more clinical. In the end, it looked more like a studio than a flower shop.

Getting back to a life simply lived, the simple flowers followed. It's not to say that this is easy. Simplicity is extremely difficult to pull off. Simplicity is elegant. It's all about attention to detail. It's still just flowers, though; it's

Parrot tulips, arranged in abundance in a green ceramic vase
PHOTO BY BRIE WILLIAMS

not rocket science. If you just learn to enjoy them, you can't possibly fail in arranging them. All the floral arrangements I've ever seen are beautiful. What? Yours is different than hers? But they're both fabulous; it doesn't matter. I think Americans are coming to the realization that there is a simple way to bring beauty to the increasingly stressful pace of life. I once had my own eyes opened by watching tulip stems come to rest—all on their own—in a perfect shape. Such a simple experience, yet full of such pleasure, joy and relief.

Analogously, look at how vital and important cooking has become. People responded to it after Julia Child pioneered in the field all those years on PBS. I like to think that her viewers started cooking together. Likewise, can you imagine sharing life, in the present, arranging a beautiful bouquet? I want to show people how to bring flowers into their culture. In Europe or Asia, people regularly buy flowers every week. Only 20 percent of Americans currently do the same, and I think it's to our disadvantage. So many of us are missing out on what flowers can do for the soul. More relaxing than yoga or a martini, more indulgent than a massage or a hair appointment, flowers can offer fun and luxury in the same breath as charm and art, beauty and simplicity.

Do you want to know where I think we are with regard to the understanding of flowers today?

We're where Julia Child was in the 1960s.

THE LOOK

I found that putting fifty stems of any one flower together made an impact. I made a rule of thumb for myself: "A lot of anything looks good." A lot of chocolate. A lot of plums.

17

Piles of coffee beans, fields of tall grasses. I also discovered, unbelievably, that abundant groupings were taking the money out of the traditional flower-arranging formula. More and more I realized it was affordable for people to arrange flowers on their own using my very simple, minimal, graphic techniques.

After working to finish an arrangement one night, I noticed bits of dirt and fertilizer on the stems. I picked up the tulips and washed them at a sink. Then I dropped them into a clear container. Quite naturally, the stems twisted.

For years, I had complained that below the waterline foliage became visually chaotic and confusing, often creating a mess of bacteria in the water—I even sought to remedy the aesthetic discomfort with tinted vases and fabric coverings. On this night, however, the stems lined up like pencils or straws in a jar. The moment crystallized everything I was looking for in my evolving style of simplicity and abundance.

Now several times a year at Flower School New York, I demonstrate how to create the same tulip bouquet. For the original, which brought me attention in 1980, I rigorously used only monochromatic white flowers. Today, the color is less important to me. We'll learn how to use this simple technique to re-create the arrangement—and many others—throughout this book. You may be surprised to learn that such bouquets are built on a table, as opposed to in a vase. We strip most of the foliage away and lay the stems out in a straight line, head to head, very neatly. What's left is the inherent beauty of the color, shape and fragrance of the flowers themselves.

A SIMPLE PATH

I did not travel the road to that powerful breakthrough technique alone. Through my own evolution as a florist and as a minimalist, my influences have evolved, as well, and I'd be remiss not to mention my gratitude for them here. After my extensive training as a child and teen with my father and his contemporaries, I looked for florists outside of that realm. In the 1950s and '60s, I much admired the floral work of Max Schling, Macdonald Forbes, Jamie Cardonna and Abel Parmentola. Later I worked at the largest flower shop in northern California: Ah Sam, located in San Mateo. There I was the teacher's pet, and Mable Ahsam gave me artistic freedom in a real, sophisticated floral operation. When I heard about a remarkable florist called C.J. Burnett in St. Petersburg, Florida, I moved there and offered my services for free. He hired me, and I learned so much. This man was a genius.

In 1980, my love of Japanese art—which had also influenced my father—came forth. I became a partner in a venture with a Japanese woman named Miho Kosuda, a perfectionist with a vast disciplined training. She refined my knowledge and taught me the Japanese sensibility.

As my own recognition in my field emerged, I began to know and be known by florists from the United States and other parts of the world. I met and spoke to many, but the one man who influenced me the most was Noboru Kurisaki. His avant-garde approach within and without the rules of

A regal arrangement of calla lilies in a metal deco vase
PHOTO BY BRIE WILLIAMS

nature created a floral style that was fresh, valued and beautiful, and I must mention him here.

"I come, but first a school" are the purported words of iconic choreographer George Balanchine upon his decision to leave Russia and usher in a revolutionary new era in American dance composition and teaching. They've inspired me during the development of my Flower School New York (www.flowerschoolny.com) classes under director Eileen Johnson. Of course, our school isn't the first for floral arranging in the country, but it may be the only one to teach a philosophy, style and technique. Professionals come to learn these; beginners enjoy a therapeutic teatime workshop emphasizing culture, civilization and beauty. All share a passion and embrace the opportunity to focus on the act of creation. For how does one fall out of love with flowers? They allow all of us to participate and understand our relationships with nature. It's as though we pass through a door from the rigors of everyday life into a larger reality.

Today my signature arrangements continue to be made with a single variety of flower in one color. The vases used, normally clear and often square, allow lithe, bending stems to capture the imagination. My method also forms the foundation of my shops called Hybrid, located in Pound Ridge and in Manhattan's elegant, anachronistic Tudor City. Going back to the 1980s, our work in the world of fashion alone has allowed association with, among others, Bill Blass, Calvin Klein, Oscar de la Renta, Dolce & Gabbana, Carole Hochman, Mollie Parnis, Valentino and Zoran. Into the 1990s through today, additional clients include Armani, Coach, Juicy Couture, Dior, Tom Ford, Gucci, Tommy Hilfiger, Michael Kors, Karl Lagerfeld, Polo Ralph Lauren, Yves Saint Laurent, Stella McCartney, Prada, Tracy Reese, Rodarte, Christian Francis Roth, Kate Spade, Versace, Victoria's Secret and Vera Wang. We have also served those in theater, music, movies, TV, print publications and other media. Michael George designs have become valued accoutrements to corporations, hotel chains, casinos, restaurants, stores, events and parties and, of course, weddings.

I will try to give you inspiration and knowledge so that you, too, can enjoy all that flowers have to offer: the simple beauty of the *quattro stagione*.

Thank you for reading my book.

Michael George

One of my classes at Flower School New York: above, left to right, students Kimberly McGah and Lisa Levy following as I demonstrate my tabletop arranging technique; below, left to right, students Anthony Markiewicz, Yukiko Otani and Siobhan Carew working to master the careful placement of their stems

PHOTOS BY MING CHANG

part one
FLORAL DESIGN

flowers in today's world

As a dress can accelerate design trends if worn to a *Vogue* shoot or the Academy Awards, flowers—both classic arrangements and newer innovations—can send volcanic reverberations of their own.

In the 1980s, the signature look I created for Calvin Klein—a simple, graphic, modern arrangement of tall white calla lilies (much like the one shown on the opposite page)—was complementary to his clean style. After enjoying wide exposure in his stores and as part of his promotional campaign, the callas and miniature callas took off, first in the fashion community and then in other aspects of American culture at that time.

Similarly, the cutting-edge dress designs of Vera Wang have given me inspiration for flower concepts over the years. One was a simple graphic bride's bouquet of black roses—really black, not almost black. We arranged pure white Akito roses and spray painted them with three coats of black lacquer. The result was extraordinary. Today, it's widely accepted that wedding florals do not have to be white stephanotis and pink roses—they can be a statement of the bride's personal style and taste, and so much more.

A Vera Wang advertisement featuring an innovative Michael George bouquet

In this chapter I will offer a very brief look at the way flowers have assimilated into American culture in recent years. Focusing on my own experiences and making no effort to be all-inclusive (that would require a book in and of itself), I'll aim to give you a better understanding of the cultural and social basis for the designs I'm about to share.

An arrangement of calla lilies that re-creates the signature look I developed for Calvin Klein

PHOTO BY BRIE WILLIAMS

THE DUTCH INVASION: IMPORTS, AVAILABILITY AND PRICE

In the 1980s, urban florists' legend had it that a white truck was circling Manhattan, as existential as a streetcar named Desire, illusory as a pirate's ghost ship. It was said its cargo always remained the same: consistent, high-quality tulips without the hand-hewn look of domestic product. When put into park, wholesalers bought the majority of the shipment at once; prices soared on the spot.

Holland is a country accustomed to the intoxicating allure of flowers: During the seventeenth century, tulip mania caused a burst financial bubble with crashed bulb prices. Undeterred, century after century, the Netherlands continued on in its reckless pursuit of the perfect bloom. The Dutch Invasion began in New York when, recognizing the unmatched beauty achieved by Dutch crop evolution, a wholesale company called Sebastian and Sons became the first to import. The virtually unknown bloom varieties were placed in its white truck in a search for high-end shops that would appreciate the product. Soon, tulips no longer brought quaint tintypes to mind. Instead, they were stopping traffic.

In the next few years, tulip resources moved out of Holland to France, Italy and South America, where lower costs attracted Dutch émigrés and their businesses. Such patterns have often been observed throughout the history of the flower and will continue to develop, whether we're talking about monarchs spending fortunes on exotic plants at Versailles or the hottest designer giving a new hybrid the right placement at Fashion Week. With regard to the Dutch tulip,

the incessant American demand necessitated that flowers come from almost every continent; today, we buy them "out of season" year round. New Zealand arrivals keep florists stocked in December; Chilean blooms fill the shelves in January.

Cost, however, is not standardized. Flowers are sold on an auction system where prices fluctuate due to demand and climate change. To get top dollar, growers may decide to sell a type of bloom during a month when it is normally hard to obtain. For example, in December, a single peony from New Zealand retails for fifteen to twenty dollars (though it must be said, they're absolutely stunning); however, during the spring, one locally grown in the Northeast sells for four to eight dollars. Whether we buy breakout tulips from a truck

or strawberries or raspberries in the supermarket off season, it all comes down to how much one is willing to pay. In March, is a seven-dollar quart of raspberries worth it? The buyer is the only person who can answer that question.

five flowers and where they grow

Hybrid typically finds the best-quality blooms in specific world markets. Buying is nonexclusive, however, and preeminence changes in accordance with growing quality concerns, as well as shipping and security costs. The following list offers a contemporary snapshot of five popular flowers, their import market and seasonal availability.

nerine lily: Holland (spring) and New Zealand (fall)

hydrangea: Holland (year-round) and South America (year-round)

miniature calla lily: California (year-round) and Holland (year-round)

large calla lily: California (year-round) and South America (year-round)

tulip: Holland (year-round), France (year-round) and the United States (year-round)

Nerine lilies PHOTO BY MING CHUNG

Hydrangea PHOTO BY CYNTHIA BLACK

Miniature calla lilies PHOTO BY BRIE WILLIAMS

Large calla lilies PHOTO BY BRIE WILLIAMS
Opposite page: White tulips PHOTO BY BRIE WILLIAMS

THE ART OF THE FLOWER MARKET

Imagine yourself with my father and me in New York's bustling Twenty-eighth Street flower market of 1955. Up and down, between storefronts and taxis, among wholesalers, shop owners and fashionistas, locally grown and greenhouse blooms—all arriving by truck—are on display: peonies, hyacinth, tulips. They're the flowers of the Northeast, stems I still prefer to work with.

I've been up with my dad since four o'clock in the morning. At age nine, I've finally convinced my father, my teacher and idol, to let me take the trip with him from southern Westchester into Manhattan. I can still close my eyes and picture myself there. Around us trucks are being unloaded with flowers from as far away as Florida and Colorado. Calls along the street peddle the latest arrivals. An old woman who winks at me when she tells jokes moves her plants into the morning sun on the sidewalk. I immediately feel at home in the flower market, and I begin riding along with my father sporadically, every few weeks. Throughout the next ten years, I'll become as much of a fixture on Twenty-eighth Street as the salty lady getting laughs.

Then, in the mid-'60s, the market changes. The product territory jumps, enlarged by a new industry transport: jet aircraft. In the exponentially expanding coast-to-coast flower market, type and availability are completely transformed; in the next decade, imports from Hawaii, South America and Mexico come to supplement a floral palette that suddenly seems virtually endless.

Today, the hottest blooms to arrange can come from as near as your local farmer's market to as far as the other side of the world.

Above and on opposite page: Choice blooms at the Twenty-eighth Street flower market in Manhattan

PHOTOS BY CYNTHIA BLACK

HOT BLOOMS TO ARRANGE TODAY

Alstroemeria

This two-toned, mass-produced flower that can be seen on every street corner has a number of very beautiful varieties and colors—including mesmerizing soft oranges, a rich purple, an unusual ruby red and a very pure white. In a tailored, graphic styling, they may remind you of butterflies, extremely full and large en masse—and they'll last up to two weeks. Buy hydroponically or homegrown blooms from Canada if the opportunity presents itself. The prices will be higher, but the alstroemeria will be at their healthiest, with large, well-developed florets at the stems. The South American varieties found at greengrocers are a more readily available and affordable option, but they're grown outdoors in less sophisticated conditions—as are most of the flowers from this part of the world. Although they'll be more tattered from exposure to the elements and dubious caretaking procedures, even this should not deter anyone from arranging the always beautiful alstroemeria in abundance.

An abundant arrangement of alstroemeria in a tall, clear, glass rectangular vase

PHOTO BY BRIE WILLIAMS

Calla Lilies

One of my clients informed me that in Venezuela these tropical flowers are considered "weeds." This, despite the attention paid to them during the art deco period by the designer Erte, painter Georgia O'Keeffe, psychoanalyst Sigmund Freud and even Katharine Hepburn, whose character in the 1937 film comedy *Stage Door* finally learns to act through the reiteration of lines beginning, "The calla lilies are in bloom again." By the time Calvin Klein asked me to design a bouquet for his 1987 collection, the flower was fast becoming an art historian's footnote and an old-fashioned choice for nuptials and funerals. My signature arrangement used many calla lilies in what looks like one outsized white blossom, perfectly dovetailed with the fashion designer's own minimalist style.

Calvin's Callas, as we called them, perfectly complemented Klein's sleek look. Today, I continue to use two thousand calla stems a week (one bouquet may have two hundred stems in it), recapturing his original arrangement, still unflinchingly modern, disorienting, perennially fascinating to the eye. For the best and most constant supply, choose Colombian product, though callas are also widely available from other South American countries, as well as Mexico, Holland, Hawaii and Jamaica. You can also find great miniature calla lilies, which were genetically created in Japan, available year-round in a wide variety of colors, from purple haze to mango, from crystal blush to parfait. Arrangements with mini callas are always cutting edge, especially with flower aficionados.

Simply elegant callas
PHOTO BY BRIE WILLIAMS

Carnations

Carnations are the perfect summer house gift, if a particularly American one. Brought out during the weekends, with refrigeration during the week, they will last from midsummer to September. In a tight minimalist bouquet of variegated blooms with a red line running through the middle, the flowers are very chic. But don't worry: I don't aim to change their synonymous relationship with Mother's Day, a father's boutonniere or even a corny green remembrance on St. Patrick's Day (in fact, I recommend that next March you try a green "Prado" carnation from Italy). Calling them by their old-fashioned names, "dianthus" or "pinks," your grandmother would have recognized carnations in a red tone and may have grown them in her yard. Italian blooms are considered superior in quality, though at half the price, the Colombian flowers are most practical. Because of their overexposure in diners and supermarkets, carnations are often known as "the flower we love to hate"—but don't let that deter you from using them. They come in hundreds of varieties, including popular minis. And according to *The American Carnation: How to Grow It* by Charles Willis Ward, they owe much to the experimentation of a botanist named W.P. Simmons. It was his personal challenge to create a pure white carnation. From 1885 through the end of the century, he obsessively engineered lighter and lighter hues of the flower, but he was never fully able to manufacture unblemished white. Always somewhere, often at the center, there was a small fleck of red. To this day the conundrum remains unresolved; tear apart a light-hued carnation and the small stain is there. Today we call this mark "Simmons's signature."

"Prado" green carnations up close
PHOTO BY BRIE WILLIAMS

For years, French roses dominated the flower market lead by the Sonja rose, named after 1920s and '30s Olympic skating star Sonja Henie. Since the mid-'90s, however, supplies have expanded, making rare English garden roses and heirloom roses from the Rockefeller gardens possible floral additions to anyone's home. Unfortunately, prices can be excessive—especially during St. Valentine's Day, when it may be wiser to choose an alternative red flower (even reliable florists will raise prices in mid-winter as their own wholesale costs increase). Also, at any time of year, don't pay unnecessarily for stem length (although roses are priced that way). In the 1930s the precious long-stemmed rose was an important consideration for buyers, largely because of the difficulty in growing it. Today, designers are more interested in the size and quality of a bloom. They're also interested in color. Roses, of course, come from all over the globe and grow in all hues, including black, a green and the successful blue, an age-old challenge to biologists. They also don't always have to be expensive. For a goodbye party or quick dinner, the eight-dollar stems aren't needed. Cheaper Ecuadorian roses might be a better choice—they're of high quality, usually grown by knowledgeable Europeans. While their stems are thicker and stiffer from being raised outdoors, the blooms are just as beautiful as any other. Recommended also are American home-garden blooms if you can find them (many such farms have been sold off, casualties of escalating real estate prices). If you can't find local stems, both Canadian and Mexican product might be considered instead.

For times that do warrant paying double the price: When the flower can be given the focus and attention it deserves, choose European blooms, from the Dutch, in particular—they know how to treat the queen. (See chapter three for my preferred technique for arranging roses.)

Large white Dutch Avalanche roses arranged in a crystal vase
PHOTO BY BRIE WILLIAMS

Chocolate Cosmos

The wild red or pink cosmos went the way of most flowers: Botanists successfully created a white variety and then took it to the opposite end of the color spectrum. Deep chocolate-colored cosmos, with blooms hardly bigger than a quarter, are the result. Rich and dark as Godiva—and in low light, virtually indistinguishable from black—these flowers boast a multisensory genetic achievement: Scientists have been able to imbue them with a chocolate fragrance. My wife and partner, Lisa, saw the flower's potential for autumn gatherings and weddings. She began asking for it in the wholesale market and using chocolate cosmos in design. Others followed her lead. Soon enough pressure was put on growers worldwide to begin supplying this bloom regularly. We prefer Dutch product because it is available in truly massive quantities. Chocolate cosmos give a freeing alternative at today's weddings, and can masterfully extend the color spectrum for any occasion.

A close look at some delicious chocolate cosmos
PHOTO BY LISA GEORGE

four blooms worth a splurge

Hydrangea PHOTO BY BRIE WILLIAMS

Garden rose PHOTO BY LISA GEORGE

Peony PHOTO BY BRIE WILLIAMS

hydrangea: Exotic, baroque colors are worth the expense—
just three stems will fill a vase.

garden rose: Isn't it great to have a rose with fragrance
again? Choose an antique variety.

peony: In October, salmon-colored blooms are especially
huge and exotic.

protea: Newer hybrids of protea are definitely splurge
worthy: exotic, large and novel.

Protea PHOTO BY BRIE WILLIAMS

41

Alstroemeria PHOTO BY LISA GEORGE Chrysanthemums PHOTO BY LISA GEORGE Gerbera daisies PHOTO BY LISA GEORGE

alstroemeria: This flower is available in a broad range of colors (try mixing them!) and looks great in abundance. Alstroemeria lasts very well.

chrysanthemum: Mums are always available, and they are long lasting. Opt for novelty varieties, like "Santini" (pictured above) and green spider mums.

gerbera daisy: This bright, modern, cheerful flower comes in every color of the rainbow.

iris: The iris is a dependable flower; the blue is crisp and the quality is fairly consistent, no matter where the stem is bought.

Irises PHOTO BY LISA GEORGE

Roses PHOTO BY LISA GEORGE

Snapdragons PHOTO BY LISA GEORGE

Solidagos PHOTO BY BRIE WILLIAMS

rose: Roses come in an overwhelming number of varieties spanning every price range. A sampling: The Austin English garden rose typically retails for ten dollars a stem, a single large-headed South American rose can be five dollars, and a dozen locally grown sweetheart roses (pictured here) might be as little as ten dollars from the greengrocer.

snapdragon: Tall and colorful, this classic garden flower is a summertime favorite.

solidago: Arrange these long-lasting stems to make an extraordinary graphic statement.

sunflower: Everyone loves sunflowers! Try novelty varieties like the "Teddy Bear" when you can find them.

"Teddy Bear" Sunflowers PHOTO BY LISA GEORGE

SELECTING AND PURCHASING CHOICE BLOOMS

My father told me, "Shop flowers like you shop vegetables."
Look at the foliage; buy them as if you were purchasing
crisp asparagus or endive. If the leaves are fresh and healthy,
then the florets will be, too. If the stems are browning or
are bruised, the blooms will reflect the damaging effects.
I also feel the stems when I'm buying. If they seem hollow,
I know that they're deteriorating and older. Inspect the heads
next. Make sure they're properly developed, but don't buy
flowers fully opened. Bruised or smashed product should
always be set aside. When arranging flowers, you need
to start with good-quality blooms to end up with a good-
quality composition.

This is not to say that floral arranging should be or need
be expensive. Of course, there are appropriate times for
Dutch roses and tulips, or for festive but higher-priced holiday
plants. Simple corner stores or supermarkets, however,
may have an excellent selection. A tip-off is presentation.
If the flowers are neatly stacked, arranged and attended,
the probability of good product increases. Ultimately it
doesn't necessarily matter if a flower is labeled "select"
or "fancy"; what's most important is a healthy flower.

Local florists might well be the ideal and easiest source
of high-quality supply, not to mention good advice. Don't
be afraid to ask them to walk you through their refrigerators.
I also recommend reputable Internet sites, but be choosy,
as it's hard to ship flowers well. My personal online choice
is www.marthastewartflowers.com.

I do not, however, advocate the average consumer
buying blooms at a flower wholesale store or district.

The reason is simple: You probably wouldn't buy meat from
a meat-packing warehouse. Flower wholesalers are prepared
to deal with store owners and industry representatives.
Other customers can be off-loaded with inferior product, rip
off pricing and bad service. Many amateur flower buyers and
arrangers will insist on having such an experience, but very
few of them ever go back for more.

No matter how you go about it, the point is to bring
flowers into our lives. Let them enter simply, with as little
stress as possible. Suddenly, you'll find that the mood of a
room seems changed. A simple arrangement can transform
a forgotten niche into a place of reflection and conversation.
With the addition of a renewable beauty, changing season
to season, guests may not know what it was like before.
They probably won't have to.

Striking anemones in subtle, variegated hues
PHOTO BY BRIE WILLIAMS

tools & tricks of the trade

Working with flowers is far simpler than most people realize. With just a basic workspace in your own home, a few essential tools and supplies, comfortable clothes and a sincere appreciation for the natural beauty of flowers, you'll have everything you need to get started. Learning to properly handle the stems is the first essential step to creating simply elegant arrangments for yourself and those around you.

A graphically styled arrangement of gentians displayed in a tall glass cylinder

PHOTO BY BRIE WILLIAMS

My workspace in my Hybrid shop in Pound Ridge, New York
PHOTO BY CYNTHIA BLACK

CREATING A WORKSPACE AND GATHERING TOOLS

To ensure adequate room to properly work with flowers, you'll need to select and clear a flat space, a minimum of about 2' x 4' (61cm x 122cm) in size, with good light. Most people prefer to work in their kitchen, particularly one with nice windows and plenty of counter space near the sink; although with a little invention, you might prefer to work outside on a porch or patio.

Most of the floral tools are fairly standard. You'll probably already have them on hand or be able to obtain them easily. Gather together:

flower-cutting and grafting tools: Many people prefer a florist's knife to scissors or like to work with both tools when cutting stems, but for beginners, I recommend scissors. If you're going to be working with roses or other woody flowers, you'll also need a grafting tool for removing thorns. Victorinox Swiss Army, Smith & Hawken, Pottery Barn, Martha Stewart and my own Flower School New York all make or sell excellent flower-cutting and grafting tools. Japanese-made tools are of high quality, but they're costly; inexpensive versions that can be found at the hardware store often work just as well.

nonmetallic vases or plastic buckets: Fill these with lukewarm water to hold your flowers prior to arranging them.

vases or other attractive containers: Carefully consider how you would like to display each arrangement. An antique vase will create a very different look from a modern glass container tinted to the bloom color or palette of your flowers, but both can be lovely in different settings. Fill your container one-half to three-quarters full with lukewarm water. For the purposes of creating the Michael George graphic look, I usually recommend a 5" x 5" (13cm x 13cm) square vase, 4" x 4" (10cm x 10cm) square vase or 5" x 5" (13cm x 13cm) cylinder to begin. Opt for clear or frosted glass, or take it to the other extreme and choose a dramatic opaque black. For tall branches, I prefer a 14" x 6" (36cm x 15cm) vase.

rubber bands or clear hair ties: Clear rubber bands that discretely hold the stems in place are the secret ingredient to achieving the signature Michael George look. Slide a band up around the stems (being careful not to hurt them by wrapping too tight) and secure them near the top of a container unobtrusively. When I developed this method I first used thin rubber bands from Italy that tied imported flowers.

Later I discovered a clear plastic hair tie that worked even better. It is designed for hair but adjusts perfectly for flowers—it disappears at the waterline. Originally found at Ricky's NYC, a beauty supply chain based in New York (www.rickys-nyc.com), these surprisingly strong and inexpensive bands have made their way into department stores and pharmacies. In a pinch, though, an ordinary rubber band will work.

Chrysal or Floralife: Always use a conditioner or preservative to increase the longevity of your arrangements. These work by giving bacteria (an inevitable part of flower arranging) an option: Instead of attacking the stems, it's able to feed on a sugary food that also feeds the flowers. I don't recommend using cane sugar, aspirin or copper pennies for florals—this is where the old wives' tales begin. Instead, try two superior products: Floralife (www.floralife.com) retards

master class

Floral tools are dangerous. Be sure to keep your cutters closed when they are not in use. Knives and scissors can easily be buried in foliage and flowers. Cleaning your workspace, you might inadvertently unearth a dangerous blade or throw a tool out altogether. Treat flower tools with a great deal of respect.

Clockwise from top: heavy-duty stapler, Chrysal, flower-cutting tool, knife, clear hair ties, rubber bands
PHOTO BY CYNTHIA BLACK

A selection of vases used at Hybrid
PHOTO BY CYNTHIA BLACK

deterioration, and Chrysal (www.chrysalusa.com) enhances plant development. Both products ease water absorption and slow bacteria growth, and both contain sugar, alum and chlorine. Though their original formulas work fine for most purposes, know that variations specifically designed for a particular type of flower group, bulb or branch are also available. Floralife and Chrysal come in containers or packets. Always add one or the other to your water prior to arranging your blooms, and each time you change the water in maintaining an arrangement.

CARING FOR FLOWERS PRIOR TO ARRANGING

Flowers arrive from the market in need of water. Technically, it's best to bring flowers home late in the day or at night so they can have approximately eight hours to absorb water, irrigate and replenish in a cool place before being arranged or displayed. Most flowers will do best refrigerated at 40°F–45°F (4°C–7°C). Orchids, jasmine, passion flowers, clematis and other tropicals, however, must be kept above 60°F (16°C)—otherwise, they will wilt and fail to develop. Freezing cold temperatures can be hazardous to any bloom; when transporting flowers in the winter, be sure to cover them.

When you obtain flowers, as soon as possible:

1] Fill a nonmetallic vase or even a plastic container about two-thirds full with water. Take the blooms, one stem at a time, and lay them on the workspace, discarding all rubber bands and paper. Loosen the stems by gently separating each bunch. If the stems have thorns, remove them (see page 54 for instructions on how to do so). Remove foliage below the waterline. If you fail to do so, bacteria will form, causing an unpleasant odor, coloring the vase water and shortening the time an arrangement will last. Leave as much greenery as possible above the waterline until you're ready to arrange the flowers.

2] Lay the flowers neatly on your workspace. If there's a variance in length, grade them, putting shorter stems to one side and taller ones to the other. Form loose pyramidal mounds as you group, keeping the heads of the flowers even. Bind flowers of similar length with a rubber band so they'll be easier to handle later.

3] Use a cutting tool to shorten the stems by ¼"–½" (about 1cm) in length. Quickly place the blooms into the prepared water containers. Add Chrysal or Floralife to the water and move the containers of flowers to a cool area, such as a refrigerator or basement (preferably 40°F–45°F [4°C–7°C]) for the night. When time is tight (if you're preparing for a dinner party that night, for instance), such rigor may not be possible. Nevertheless, proper irrigation does ensure that your flowers will last five to fifteen days without compromise. (Some, such as chincherinchee, can last up to a month with proper care.)

The addition of floral food, a step that should never be skipped to ensure healthy, long-lasting flowers
PHOTO BY CYNTHIA BLACK

HANDLING FLOWERS LIKE A PRO

Always be gentle with flowers when cleaning them. Resist the urge to overhandle the stems, as doing so can damage them. This is especially true with white flowers and those with delicate petals, like tulips. Handle your blooms with the utmost care. Never sit them in direct sunlight or on hot or cold surfaces for any length of time. Resist the urge to pack blooms tightly into any container, especially when storing them before arranging; give them room to relax as they drink. Finally, whenever handling your flowers, whether cleaning or arranging them, do quality control on each stem as you work, using your fingers to gently remove any broken or bruised foliages or petals.

When it comes time to arrange your stems, be sure to recut them as you work—this assures that the flowers will be able to drink their water easily and will last as long as possible. Typically, when it comes time to create an arrangement I'll strip all the stems completely of their foliage—as you proceed through this book, you won't see a lot of greenery in signature Hybrid arrangements. If you prefer a look that's not so graphic, though, you can certainly allow some greens to arrange—many other acclaimed florists do. For bulb flowers, about 1"–3" (3cm–8cm) of top greenery is typical.

The most popular flower that requires any special preparation beyond these simple steps is the rose. Because their stems are woody and thorny, and because roses have a tendency to become air blocked by the time you get them home to arrange them, there are some basic tricks of the trade you should know for preparing and caring for these stems prior to arranging them. These are outlined for you with simple instructions and photographs on the following pages.

Otherwise, if handling your flowers like a professional sounds relatively simple, that's because it is. And once you follow the proper procedures for handling and caring for the stems, the hard-and-fast rules of flower arranging stop there. What you choose to do in creating your arrangement depends on your personal taste, and the look you're trying to create for the occasion the bouquet is intended for. In chapter three, I will teach you the basic techniques that make up the foundation for my own flower work.

master class

Every third day, the stems of all arrangements should be rinsed, and the vases filled with fresh water and Chrysal or Floralife.

Tall and sturdy young snowball viburnum, the blooms of which turn white upon maturity, displayed in a tall crystal vase
PHOTO BY BRIE WILLIAMS

TRICK OF THE TRADE:
preparation of roses

Working with the beautiful yet particular rose requires a
bit more preparation than working with less woody stems.

1   Remove all foliage below the intended
    waterline and dethorn the stems, as shown
    here. To do so, stand the rose on the table.
    Using the flat side, not the sharp edge,
    of a grafting tool, work straight down the
    stem, spinning the flower and carefully
    removing every thorn. Be careful not to
    tear the skin. Work slowly until you've
    mastered the technique.

2   Clean the head of each bloom by taking off
    the thick outside petal, called the shipping
    leaf (it's used to protect the more tender
    inner petals). Be sure not to peel away
    too many layers of petals—it will give
    the bouquet a nub-like appearance. For a
    gardenesque feel for an arrangement, leave
    the outer layer on.

PHOTOS BY CYNTHIA BLACK

Demand for more interesting flowers has led consumers to become increasingly aware of the wide range of color available in roses, as well as their three forms.

CUP

You'll recognize this form as the traditional rose. Consumers have been accustomed to buying these blooms over the years, as evidenced by the timeless popularity of the American Beauty rose. Cup roses have elongated heads and lower petal counts than some other varieties.

BOWL

These squat flowers are plump, not long, and have a high petal count, which is one of the ways professionals gauge the desirability of a rose. Roses with high petal counts will be showier as they open—and will last longer, too. Thus, bowl roses are often preferred by experienced flower arrangers.

SAUCER

Flatter, camellia-like garden varieties of roses tend to have this form. The Austin, an English garden rose, is a good example of the saucer rose.

TRICK OF THE TRADE:

restoring air-blocked roses

Because of their woody stems, roses have a more difficult time absorbing water and getting initial irrigation after being cut (especially if they've been left out of water for any length of time). Although the blooms themselves look fine, some will flop over due to a phenomenon called air block. Here is the Ikebana technique to restore them: Boiling water is poured to shock the flowers. The air rushes out of the stems, and the water is allowed to go straight to the head, in a siphon effect.

materials

air-blocked roses

container or vase of cool water

Chrysal or Floralife rose food

boiling water

grafting tool

florist's knife and/or scissors

tape or a stapler

ceramic or glass container (a coffee cup works in a pinch)

large sheet of paper for wrapping stems, if they did not come wrapped from the store or florist

1   Remove thorns and foliage as shown on page 54.

2   Bind the roses together with a rubber band at least 6" (15cm) above their bottoms.

3   Cover the flowers by creating a paper cone around them (using the wrapping in which they've been brought home from the florist or store is fine). Exposing approximately 6" (15cm) of the stems, tape and staple the cone, being careful not to puncture or otherwise injure the stems.

4   Cut the stems approximately ½" (1cm) at the bottom, straight and clean, and place the bunch in a small heat-resistant container.

5   Boil water in a tea kettle or in the microwave. Pour boiling water into the container until it's about 1"–1½" (3cm–4cm) deep and the stems are submerged.

6   Leave the flowers in the water until the water becomes tepid (3–5 minutes). You'll see bubbles coming out of the bottoms where the air was blocked.

7   Remove the roses from the water, take off the paper and thrust the stems into deep, clean, cool water with Chrysal or Floralife rose food. Place the container of flowers in a cool area as close to 45°F (7°C) as possible.

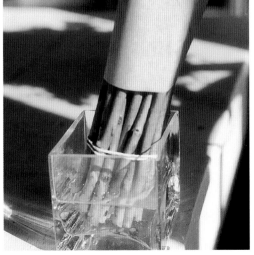

signature flower arranging techniques

Flowers, of course, know they look good. We don't have to teach them anything. Put them in the sun and water them, and they'll develop, ultimately going to seed, trying to procreate as expediently as possible. Of course, along the way, they don't mind being treated gently, admired, talked to and, some even say, sung to …

In this chapter I will introduce my two key signature techniques for arranging flowers: the Hybrid Tabletop Technique, in which the bouquet is built on a flat surface and then transferred, finished, to a vase; and the Hybrid Matrix Technique, in which the arrangement is built in the container that will display it. When working with flowers that are short and are to be placed in a low bowl—or with blooms that have repetitive structures—you will have greater success with the Hybrid Tabletop Technique, which creates a neat arrangement with the stems cleanly aligned. When working with flowers that are tall and varied in their faces and the shapes of their stems, you should generally opt for the Hybrid Matrix Technique,

which weaves even the most awkward of stems together in a way that holds them perfectly in place.

You can certainly experiment with mixing and matching different types of flowers with the two techniques to determine what feels right to you and what works best for the look you wish to create. Rules are made to be broken, and you will certainly find evidence throughout this book of my own experimentation—arranging woody lilac stems with the Hybrid Tabletop Technique, for instance (see page 86).

Once you master the Tabletop and Matrix techniques, you'll find you can apply them universally to endless types of flowers, creating literally hundreds of graphic arrangements, all very different in appearance but based on the same core principles of floral design. I'll reference them in the pages ahead without always repeating all of the instructions and steps, but please refer to this chapter anytime you need a detailed refresher.

Green dendrobium orchids suspended in a tall crystal vase
PHOTO BY BRIE WILLIAMS

the hybrid tabletop technique

When a type of flower has long stems that are straight but flexible, it can often be difficult to coax the blooms into formation in a vase. They'll simply lean or bend whichever way they please. The Hybrid Tabletop Technique resolves this common problem and ensures that the resulting composition will be graphic and clean. Try this technique on simple flowers that look good in abundance, like these hyacinths. Your friends and family will be wondering how you got the arrangement so perfect on your first try.

concept:

1 Using a tabletop or other flat work surface, work with cleaned flowers to create the foundation of a pyramid. Lay the blooms down next to each other evenly. Place the tallest straight stems in the middle.

2 Nestle new rows on the previous lines of flowers. As neatly as possible, overlap the stems, building to an apex.

prepare:

12 hyacinths blooms (white, blue or personal preference)

vase filled ½–¾ full with lukewarm water and Chrysal or Floralife

florist's knife or scissors

small rubber band or clear hair tie

create:

TECHNIQUE: Hybrid Tabletop

CONTAINER OF CHOICE: 4" × 3" (10cm × 8cm) clear rectangular container

master class

There is a natural but unnecessary tendency to dome down while building out. Instead, just try and make a straight line across the top with the heads. Keep the stems at the base gathered together; let the tops spread out.

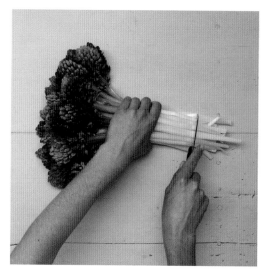

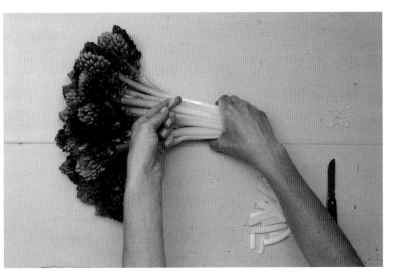

1 Remove the hyacinths from their packaging; rinse the stems of all sand and dirt. Gently strip away foliage and use a cutting tool to shorten the stems by ¼"–½" (about 1cm) in length.

2 Choose one straight, strong hyacinth to become the center post of your arrangement and lay it on the table. One by one, begin adding flowers to form a line. Place right-leaning stems to the right of the center, and left-leaning stems to the left.

3 Build up a pyramidal structure of hyacinths, nestling stems in between each other, steadily mounding upward. Try to align the heads of the blooms as much as possible, not worrying about the lengths of the stems— you'll cut them later.

4 When you are happy with the way the flowers are aligned, grasp stems together in your nondominant hand, holding them tightly in position, and trim the ends flush with your cutting tool.

5 Still grasping the stems in their perfectly aligned position, use the thumb and forefinger of your dominant hand to stretch open a rubber band or clear hair tie. Slide it up the stems to band them together.

6 Pick the flowers up and take an eyeball measurement of their height against the container you've chosen. Trim the stems flush as necessary so that the blooms will rise just above the container. Adjust the band so it will fall just at the waterline, where it will be least obtrusive.

7 Grasp the stems firmly in both of your hands as shown and, with your bottom hand, twist the stems as your top hand gently resists the motion. The result should be a perfectly clean, aligned twist.

master class

When you are first learning this technique, you may need a helper to band the stems while you hold them in position with both of your hands. When you are more experienced, you can use this technique to build a larger arrangement with forty to fifty stems—and having someone to help you will come in handy then, too, as you cut and band the stems. Don't forget to breathe—or to observe the simple graphic elegance of a classic bloom.

8 Cut the stems once more if necessary to ensure the bottom of the arrangement will be perfectly flush and sit evenly in your vase. Place the arrangement in water and primp.

PHOTOS BY BILL MILLER

the hybrid matrix technique

If arrangements for roses and other woody, thick-stemmed flowers are created on the table, too many flowers are inevitably used. And with the uneven stems being forced into unnatural alignment, the resulting arrangement will look stiff. The small imperfections that come by putting the blooms together in a matrix, however, will make the finished dome-shaped design more beautiful and natural looking.

concept:

1   Using a round or square container, work in a clockwise fashion, placing each flower stem underneath the preceding one and leaning them at angles against the container's sides.

2   After the first, outer row has been established, place the next blooms in a counterclockwise pattern. Each should lean naturally against the first row and nestle neatly under the stem. This process will create a matrix for the rest of the flowers to be placed in—and allow the arranger a large degree of control.

3   Fill voids by placing flowers where needed.

4   Save a straight, especially beautiful flower for the center.

prepare:

24–26 roses in various shades of pink

vase filled ¾ full with lukewarm water and Chrysal or Floralife

grafting tool

florist's knife and/or scissors

create:

TECHNIQUE: Hybrid Matrix

CONTAINER OF CHOICE: 5" × 5" (13cm × 13cm) clear glass cylinder or square

1   Remove foliage and thorns from the roses, as explained on page 54. Clean the head of each rose by taking off the thicker outside shipping leaf.

2   Cut the first rose and lean it against the side of the container, so that the head is separated from the edge of the vase by about 1" (3cm).

3   Go around the container in a clockwise fashion, leaning each stem diagonally underneath the one before it until 8–9 blooms have been placed in the vase, forming an outer ring.

4   Now begin a second circle just inside the first, working counterclockwise and leaning the stems back in the opposite direction, one stem supporting the other, until another ring of 8 roses has been created. By this time the matrix, the stem configuration, very neat and logical through the clear glass, should be apparent. Notice that the flowers are starting to form a dome.

5   Work clockwise and, in opportune spots, fill in the arrangement. When you are working in a container this small, the third ring may not be a ring at all, but simply a center section positioned in the same careful way as the outer circles to complete the dome shape.

When almost all 24–26 of your blooms have been placed, work a little more loosely, adding flowers as needed to fill in any holes in the dome. The overall effect should be balanced, symmetrical and mechanical.

6   Place a beautiful, straight rose in the middle to become the peak of your dome, which should be low, squat and wide, unlike a cone.

master class

Creating a matrix in a square or rectangular container, after you create the first outer row, you may want to cut the rest of the flowers' stems just a bit shorter to maintain a tailored appearance as you form the inner rows of the arrangement. Even with less length than the outer stems, when these flowers are arranged in the matrix design, you can easily coax them into standing up more vertically to fill out the dome shape properly.

THE WALK

Right in front of your eyes are the found materials of the *quattro stagione*. They're the flowers in our backyards, at our local florists or along wooded paths. They're the inspiration, here today, forever lost in a week. In many instances their bulbs and roots will continue to thrive, completing one cycle, anticipating another. The blossoms themselves, however, may be left unnoticed, missed entirely. Wherever you are, in this minimal space between technique and execution, dream such blooms into being seen. Call it planning—imagine you want to adorn your home with just the right combination of flowers for a party—or name it conjuring—put yourself in your guest's shoes and begin.

Pause at the front door to observe and "feel" your reception area or foyer. As you consider a space for flowers, start with a pad and pencil, noting where appointments should be made. Discern where they're needed naturally given the home's architecture and furnishings. Follow the likely pathway of guests at a party or gathering, and soon you'll be in the right mindset to consider practical matters as well as aesthetics. Think of variables such as lighting, the size of the home, whether it's in the country or city, the season, flower availability, prices, plant height and even whether or not strong scents would be welcome. A vase or container, perhaps a family heirloom, might come to mind that should be used. Imagine the seasonal flower, branch—from quince to dogwood and blueberry—or foliage that might be placed in it.

Calla lilies command attention on display
PHOTO BY BRIE WILLIAMS

The coats have now been taken and guests are asked about cocktails. Continue the route and pause at the doorway of the sitting room, viewing the entire space, every surface and window. We might find one or two high tables with lamps, a couch, club chairs around a low coffee table, perhaps, and maybe a side table with a mirror or painting. The coffee table will receive the most important decoration in the room, normally a low-domed arrangement—peonies, anemones, callas, tulips—that should be unobtrusive and elegant. Let the flowers here lend themselves not only to the décor but also to the beginning communication at the party: "Look at them—double white tulips from France." Flowers are wonderful to talk about socially because oftentimes we can agree that they're beautiful.

The mantel lends itself to small but important objects in pairs. Perhaps small square containers with subtle, graphic, English ivy topiaries, or small potted flowers placed in vases. On the high tables with lamps, a julep cup might contain only a touch of flower, an anemone, for example. You might find the sideboard is the right spot for a tall phalaenopsis orchid that's contemporary, long lasting and simple.

Continue your walk to the dining room, where you may have three or more arrangements on a long table. Go into the bath, where a green or orange chincherinchee, a modest bloom also called star of Bethlehem and often used for men, or a scented flower such as hyacinth would be enjoyable to find. Move to the patio where clay-potted flowers welcome you. The point as you plan is not to overdecorate or to let the florals become intrusive. Don't ask blooms to compete with each other, with the attention of your guests or with a stunning vista. They need to be ever-present, understated, always within eyeshot. Flowers should offer a different inhabitation, reminding us of luxury and moments of sublime beauty, taking us outside of ourselves.

Bright spring ranunculus, arranged in a sleek, short black glass cylinder for an ultramodern look
PHOTOS BY BRIE WILLIAMS

part two
QUATTRO STAGIONE

MARCH NOTEBOOK

Dreaming of spring: Weeks before winter ends, spring graces the covers of catalogs and magazines, and these flowers appearing in our mailboxes and on newsstands make us long for the change of the seasons. Then, seemingly overnight, color. Yellow is often the first hue, chasing the cold and darkness away as the forsythia, daffodil and crocus awaken. Watch for the freshest flowers coming into florists and grocers; you'll be delighted one day to be greeted by new pastel splashes of the tulip, muscari, hyacinth and lilac. Lining the streets, budding maple, hickory, oak, birch and catalpa further announce spring's arrival. Cut a blossoming dogwood branch; inside, you can watch it develop for further inspiration. We'll start with the simplest of seasonal arrangements—lily of the valley. Then, throughout the year, we'll move on to more advanced designs. Bouquets, like the oldest of friends, always share something new, even when you've

spent time with them many times before. In this time of birth, of great rejuvenation, with the temperature and scent of the air changing, we are both one with the past and with the new year's daybreak.

Hyacinths in fresh colors perfect at springtime
PHOTO BY BRIE WILLIAMS

75

lily of the valley bouquet

Harbingers of spring though they may be, you can find beautiful and delicate lily of the valley six months of the year at your local florist, available both in white and in a rare lavender color. Give this flower, as a bouquet, to a junior bridesmaid in a wedding procession or display it, as an arrangement, to reinvigorate a family room or dining table. Make no attempt to stylize the bells; lily of the valley arrangements should be kept simple, neat and tailored.

prepare:

15–18 lily of the valley stems

water glass or small round vase ½ filled with lukewarm water and Chrysal or Floralife

florist's knife and/or scissors

small rubber band or clear hair tie

create:

TECHNIQUE: Hybrid Matrix

CONTAINER OF CHOICE: ordinary water glass

master class

The Hybrid Matrix Technique can be used even for an arrangement that you want to bind into a handheld bouquet. Simply build the arrangement in the vase using the technique, then carefully remove it with both hands and use a small rubber band or clear hair tie to bind the stems into position together. You can also bind the arrangement in this manner for display in a vase if you prefer the slighly more controlled, finished look it creates.

For a surprisingly stylish and modern approach, try cutting the stems of the bound bouquet at an angle. Choose what will look best for your bouquet's final purpose.

1   Gather your lilies of the valley in one hand and, to keep the stems at equal lengths, trim their bottoms all at once with scissors or a florist's knife. Gently separate each floret stem from its foliage. Trim each floret stem and each foliage stem just a little bit more, being careful to preserve its length. Place the floret stems in a glass of water, and leave the foliage on your work surface. Using the Hybrid Matrix Technique, begin creating the outer ring with the floral stems.

2   Build the second ring using the foliage rather than the blooms. Using the Hybrid Matrix Technique, work counterclockwise and position the stems in between and behind the flowers of the first ring, standing the foliage a bit more vertically than the blooms in the outer ring.

3   Continue building the bouquet inward, alternating rings between blooms and foliage. As you move closer to the center, stand the stems up straighter to add height in the middle of the arrangement.

4   If you find holes or spaces anywhere, fill them in to complete your arrangement.

5   Forming a triangle with your thumbs and forefingers, gently lift the flowers out of the water at the top of the stems: This will pull the bouquet together.

6   Make a ring with the thumb and forefinger of your nondominant hand to hold the stems just under the blossoms, and with your free hand, slide a small rubber band or clear hair tie more than halfway up the stems.

7   Cut the bottoms of the stems flush with your florist's knife or scissors for a clean finish.

classic calla lilies

This clean arrangement is a slightly understated variation of my classic Calvin's Callas design. The original was an elegant bouquet created for a fashion show to accompany a Calvin Klein wedding dress. Later it evolved into an extravagant arrangement of more than two hundred callas for display in his Manhattan storefront. This version is a more accessible arrangement you can create for any occasion to welcome spring properly.

prepare:

25–50 calla lily stems

florist's knife and/or scissors

vase ½ filled with lukewarm water and Chrysal or Floralife

create:

TECHNIQUE: Hybrid Tabletop

CONTAINER OF CHOICE: tall glass 8" × 18" (20cm × 46cm) cylindrical vase

master class

Calla lilies are bendable and allow shaping for expressive soft lines (unlike tulips or carnations, which have brittle stems). If you use a good amount of them and employ the Hybrid Tabletop Technique, you won't even need a rubber band to bind the arrangement's clean lines.

PHOTOS BY BRIE WILLIAMS

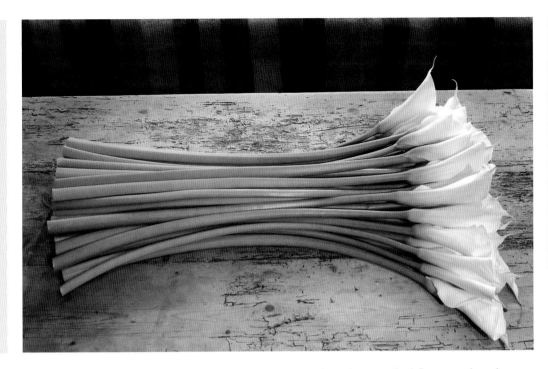

master class

Interestingly, bulbs grow at an equal rate to one another under the same conditions. Blooms grown yourself or purchased from the same grower, therefore, always remain at a similar point of development. This is enormously helpful as we arrange them — using the Hybrid Tabletop Technique, they'll fall into place quite easily.

1   Carefully unwrap the calla lilies. Hold each between the forefinger and middle finger of your nondominant hand, and gently pull the fingers of your opposite hand down each stem to shape it into a straight line or an elegant, very slight curve. Stack the shaped flowers as you work so you can see that they will align well with each another.

2   With stems this long and flexible, it may be nearly impossible to select a strong, straight stem to serve as the starting point of your arrangement, as you normally would with the Hybrid Tabletop Technique. Instead, you may find it easier to adapt your method a bit and begin by shaping four strong stems to start, choosing two that curve naturally to the left and two that lean to the right. Lay them in position on your work surface.

3   Begin building your arrangement in accordance with the Hybrid Tabletop Technique, carefully adding flowers in a straight, elegant line, placing each according to whether it naturally leans to the right or to the left. Remember, the dome shape of the final bouquet will happen naturally, so there is no need to force them into a rounded dome.

4   In a pyramid-like formation, nestle the blossoms in between one another. Once a certain width is established, build a second tier. Keep the flowers symmetrical, tops flat. Keep building. Place the stems in a way so that they fit into the grouping. Don't force them or try to balance them rigidly.

5   Eyeball the height of the vase you intend to use. Holding the stems in place with your nondominant hand, use a florist's knife to cut them all flush. With an arrangement this large, you may find it difficult to twist the stems in your hand. Either enlist a partner to help you twist them—each of you holding the arrangement in both hands—or simply maneuver them into your vase and coax them into a bit of a twist as they come to rest.

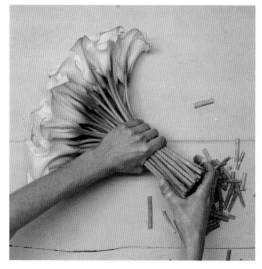

VARIATION: YELLOW MINIATURE CALLAS

To create a smaller, warmer version of the classic calla arrangement, arrange twenty miniature calla lilies using the Hybrid Tabletop Technique and transfer them to a small vase. Miniature callas are available in a wide array of colors, from a cheerful yellow fitting for springtime to shades of dramatic purple-red perfect for autumn ambiance. They may be smaller than the classic calla, but you'll find their effect is no less stunning.

FIRST DAY OF SPRING

Lilacs, crocuses, daffodils and peonies are all much anticipated after the long, hard winter. Isn't it heaven to see the earth waking up?

EASTER

The traditions are fading with time, but most will recall hyacinths, tulips, daffodils and lilies surrounding egg hunts, straw baskets and chocolate rabbits. Florists dubbed the Easter lily a religious flower in the 1940s. In actuality, the plant became popular at Easter because it could easily be transported north via truck from Florida and could be forced to bloom in hot houses; otherwise, we'd call the Bermuda lily by its real name. Today, celebrate Easter with my favorites, tulips and hyacinths.

MOTHER'S DAY

Carnations: so pretty, such humility. If the mother is alive, give colored varieties; if not, choose white blooms. Or celebrate with lilacs or peonies, the ultimate "new" flowers for Mom.

Hyacinths PHOTO BY CYNTHIA BLACK

Carnations PHOTO BY CYNTHIA BLACK

Lilacs in abundance, with their woody stems mingling in a clean twist
PHOTO BY BRIE WILLIAMS

minimal graphic tulip bouquet

Hybrid's early minimal graphic achievement: Simply using the standard Hybrid Tabletop Technique, this arrangement can be made with many spring bulb flowers, such as hyacinth, scilla, muscari, daffodil and Nerine lily. Limit yourself at least once, however, to making the arrangement the way it was originally envisioned in the early 1980s—with tulips in only one shade.

prepare:

30–50 tulips in one color

vase filled ½–¾ full with cold water and Chrysal or Floralife

florist's knife and/or scissors

rubber band or clear hair tie

gloves (optional; I wear them only because of a tulip allergy)

create:

TECHNIQUE: Hybrid Tabletop

CONTAINER OF CHOICE: modern glass vase, clear (as shown at right) or colored (as shown on opposite page)

master class

Strive for perfection always. Here, filling in the middle of a tulip pyramid, build up the center. Trust that even in the stringent minimalism of the arrangement the final effect will appear carefree. Your flowers will seem relaxed and dégagé.

Another approach to tulips: mixing bolder parrot
tulips in shades of pink and yellow

MONOCHROMATIC COMPOSITIONS

Never be afraid to mix types of flowers. A good way to begin is with a monochromatic arrangement that incorporates different blooms of the same color palette. Here I used the Hybrid Tabletop Technique to create a stunning arrangement of blue hyacinth and muscari, which are sometimes referred to as "grape hyacinth." When combining blooms of different sizes using this technique, as you create the arrangement on your tabletop, simply lay the smaller blooms (in this case, the muscari) so they will portrude above the larger ones.

highlight: hyacinths

The quintessential spring flower in the West, often brought inside at Easter; in Iran, hyacinths symbolize the New Year. Their sweet fragrance and jubilant colors—blues, pinks, purples and whites among them—force primary growers, local as well as Dutch, to offer flowers in different growth stages. For events, buy opened blooms; for gifts, present the hyacinths just cut from bulbs (they typically come in packs of twenty-five), or combine them with another flower in a similar color, as with the muscari here.

If it's possible, observe and appreciate the flowers and their developmental beauty. What starts as tight, green and unformed—hardly blooms at all—will metamorphose into multiflorets, fully opened, and always perfect for graphic composition. The transition gives us the opportunity to decipher the secrets of a bloom, if we are wise enough to engage. Many assume flowers are interesting only for a few days and are then best tossed out, their purpose in our lives completed. Better, however, is to watch this other life cycle, giving nuanced enjoyment over the course of many days, from the hyacinth's early entry into phototropism on through fruition. A hyacinth plant highlighted in its pot can be just as beautiful as an arrangement of cut stems.

NOTES ON SPRING FLOWERS AND BRANCHES

For a further look at arranging some of the most popular seasonal spring flowers, consider using Hybrid's arranging techniques with one or more of the following beautiful blooms.

clematis: Very expensive, but long lasting and beautiful, these exotic flowers should be arranged cascading in a tall, fluted vase. While they're fabulous for topping off a composition design, they are not easy to work with alone. Nevertheless, if you can master the art of arranging this flower, the results are well worth the effort.

daffodil: These happy spring blooms are reasonably priced and can be bought locally in season.

hyacinth: Local or imported Dutch blooms are available six months of the year, though imports are at least 50 percent more expensive.

lilac: The Dutch product offered year-round is virtually perfect, but it offers little fragrance. It's also more costly than American lilacs grown locally, which you'll find available only in the spring.

lily of the valley: Many think this flower defines spring, and its cost is most reasonable then. Out of season, it can be expensive.

Clematis PHOTO BY BRIE WILLIAMS

Daffodils PHOTO BY BRIE WILLIAMS

Lilies of the valley PHOTO BY BRIE WILLIAMS

Hyacinths PHOTO BY BRIE WILLIAMS

Lilacs PHOTO BY BRIE WILLIAMS

muscari (grape hyacinth): These very delicate, petite flowers should be arranged in high quantities to make an impression.

Nerine lilies PHOTO BY MING CHUNG

Peony

Ranunculus PHOTO BY BRIE WILLIAMS

nerine lily: Hybrids of this special flower can be imported from Holland and New Zealand and are long lasting.

peony: The queen of flowers is available locally in the spring; imported from New Zealand in the fall.

ranunculus: Available from California, Holland, France and local growers, these stems are reasonably priced.

sweet pea: An ever-widening spectrum of colors and constant improvement of quality are making sweet peas a favorite. They're available six months of the year locally as well as imported from France, Italy and Holland.

Sweet peas

Cherry branch

Pear branch

Forsythia branch

trees: Dogwood, cherry, forsythia and pear branches (above right) are best bought locally in season. (Some product is shipped out of season from California, but its quality can be average.) Fortunately, branch material is long lasting and, in terms of decorating, will cover a large area. Don't use too many stems, however, or you will lose the beautiful lines of the wood. Keep arrangements tall and simple, mimicking how they appear in nature.

master class

When creating springtime arrangements, combine foliage—geranium, dusty miller, hop and lady's mantle—with garden flowers like pansies and ranunculus. You'll discover timeless favorites, cool, smooth textures, shades of white ... hours gone without enough time to finish.

A spring woodland bouquet of pansies,
geranium foliage and ranunculus

PHOTOS BY BRIE WILLIAMS

Woodland flowers andromeda and helleborus combine to create a full,
fresh arrangement

PHOTOS BY BRIE WILLIAMS

Two inexpensive, simple and graphic arrangements: two-toned parrot tulips (opposite page, at left; and below at left and right) and chincherinchee (opposite page, at right; and below at center)

PHOTOS BY BRIE WILLIAMS

chapter five

due – summer

JULY NOTEBOOK

Along the back roads, summer's bounty—her crops. Farm flowers and greenhouse-grown dahlias—such color and humble informality. Zinnias, snapdragons—spiked shapes, beloved by children and adults alike, blossoming from the bottom up. Unlike spring flowers, these will take time to come to fruition. We'll see them through July and August, and even into September.

Cosmos, delphiniums, roses, carnations, gladiolas and van Gogh's sunflowers—out here in the heat and horseflies. Eremurus and butterfly bush, misrepresented as "common" flowers. The same is true for the "scrub" and "weeds" along the highway—no wonder we hear so little of nonflorals, the foliages and herbs. Scented and variegated geranium, dusty miller, lamb's ear, sage, oregano, rosemary, lavender, as well as the seedpods of spring flowers and arrays of new decorative greens from South America. They've started small, only buds and stems. Now they'd decorate a palace.

A summer Tuscan bouquet of peonies, "Blushing Bride" protea, large hybrid protea, amaranthus and seasonal foliages
PHOTOS BY BRIE WILLIAMS

hydrangea

In the summer, hydrangea, grown locally across most of the country, is not cost prohibitive—and its colors and patterns can be as unexpected as you like. Try reds, speckles, greens, yellows, pastels and whites; for quiet moments, blues and violets. Just a few blooms give plenty of coverage, and beautifully full arrangements can be built using either the Hybrid Tabletop Technique (as shown below) or the Hybrid Matrix Technique (as shown on the opposite page).

PHOTO BY LISA GEORGE

prepare:

5–8 white hydrangea blooms

vase ½ filled with lukewarm water and Chrysal or Floralife

florist's knife and/or scissors

rubber band or clear hair tie

create:

TECHNIQUE: Hybrid Tabletop

CONTAINER OF CHOICE: 5" × 4" (13cm × 10cm) rectangular vase

Opposite page: Tall hydrangea stems intertwined using the Hybrid Matrix Technique PHOTO BY BRIE WILLIAMS

ABOVE: PHOTOS BY BILL MILLER

109

highlight: hydrangea

Shaking off its identification with musty Victoriana, the hydrangea has come to help define contemporary taste. Its reborn popularity was aided, unsurprisingly, by Dutch growers. In fact, the re-emergence of this flowering bush followed a typical pattern: technologically masterminded in Japan, fine-tuned and bred in Holland, and now grown in profusion the world over.

PHOTO BY LISA GEORGE

These massive blossoms, which develop in virtually any color, may grow to be a head-turning ten inches (twenty-five centimeters) in diameter. For gifts and arrangements, though, the five-inch (thirteen-centimeter) heads are more appropriate and cost less.

The hydrangea stem itself has even been deconstructed. Although it's still thick, if not woody, newer varieties allow water to be absorbed more easily without irrigation or longevity concerns. Hydra, of course, means "water" in Greek, and it will probably always be important to keep stems immersed. If they're left out for even an hour, the petals and structure will show signs of decline. Overheating, direct sunlight or extreme cold will also make the flowers collapse. Although the delicate hydrangea can be rehydrated or even re-refrigerated, bloom damage will remain noticeable.

Distinctive year-round markets have evolved in Chile, New Zealand, France and Columbia. In the United States blooms are available through the spring and summer in early- and late-blooming varieties. If pricing sometimes seems exorbitant, recall the bloom size, which can quickly fill vases. The blossoms also need quite a bit of space and time to develop; the longer any flower has to stay in a greenhouse, the more expensive it is. Keep them as cool as possible, use flower food and give them a fresh cut when arranging.

PHOTO BY LISA GEORGE

MEMORIAL DAY

Whether you're opening a summer house or stuck in town, the unofficial start of summer calls for hydrangea. What color, what memories, what bliss!

FOURTH OF JULY

Arrange red and white carnations using the Hybrid Tabletop Technique and display them in a casual container—a cobalt blue vase, perhaps—or style them as a centerpiece in a clear vase on a Navy cloth. The marbleized effect is as bold and bright as fireworks and the flag. Keep them cool, and they'll last for weeks.

LABOR DAY

Say goodbye to summer with sunflowers. You might not have the chance to be this carefree for almost a whole year, so go wild—arrange them loosely and creatively. Or create a graphic bouquet, if you insist—either way, you can't go wrong.

dahlias

Bright, colorful and reasonably priced, dahlias are perfect in a graphic, abundant presentation. Choose from many varieties—and buy local. The key to employing the Hybrid Tabletop Technique successfully in arranging dahlias is to focus on forming a straight top edge with the blossoms. The result will be a clean, full bloom line.

prepare:

30–75 dahlias

vase ½–¾ filled with lukewarm water and Chrysal or Floralife

florist's knife and/or scissors

rubber band or clear hair tie

create:

TECHNIQUE: Hybrid Tabletop

CONTAINER OF CHOICE: 5" × 5" (13cm × 13cm) cylinder

PHOTOS BY BILL MILLER

SUMMER FOLIAGE AND HERBS

As a child in my father's store, I watched the florists work with classic foliages—huckleberry, lemon, rhododendron and leather ferns. Sweeping the cuttings—along with folding boxes for deliveries and covering the floor with sawdust so no one slipped—was a part of any flower shop apprenticeship. But my favorite cuttings to sweep came from the herb bouquets being made of fragrant oregano, rosemary, thyme and sage, heightening the senses' delight.

Although apprentices still sweep floors, of course, there is more range to the products available today, with some greens rivaling blooms in their patterns and exquisite beauty. Geranium, for example, comes in numerous varieties: dark and light, variegated and scented. Dusty miller and silver mound are also favorites of mine. And I'm currently receiving foliages from Peru that I've never even seen before! I clean the bottoms of the stems and arrange them as they grow on the plant, using nature as my guide. Once you've created a base, you can artistically insert other items—such as berries, seedpods, herbs and even flowering herbs, like oregano.

A modern arrangement of silver mound
PHOTO BY CYNTHIA BLACK

114

Experiment with summer foliage and herbs in your arrangements; the possibilities are endless. For inspiration, try browsing gardening publications—or take to your own garden and see what survives after cutting. Depending on your region, you might want to begin by gathering cedar and budding andromeda. Add hydrangea, which typically grow so big they need to be cut back. The bouquets you'll assemble will be long lasting but must be kept clean. Wash the stems and change the water at least every other day, and they'll last up to six weeks.

From top: An herbal basket of mint, thyme, flowering oregano, white rambling roses and green vibernum PHOTO BY TANYA TRIBBLE
A simple arrangement of Peruvian seedpods PHOTO BY CYNTHIA BLACK

A summer herbal bouquet including rosemary, oregano and lavender along with geranium, seedpods and seasonal foliage in a wide stone vase

PHOTOS BY BRIE WILLIAMS

116

parisian bouquet

In Paris, street vendors wrap seasonal herbs in newspaper. The Dutch call this a Biedermeier bouquet. You might make one yourself as you wander through your own garden, clipping what's freshest, gravitating freely toward whatever catches your eye—and what best celebrates a joyful mood. Abandon all techniques and build the arrangement freeform in your hands.

prepare:

FLOWERS OF CHOICE: at least 10 stems each of hydrangea (we chose blooms with a whitish-blue coloring); lace cap hydrangea (lavender); and/or sedum (choose green, undeveloped buds)

HERBS OF CHOICE: at least 10 stems each of rosemary, lavender, feverfew and/or chamomile

BERRIES OF CHOICE: at least 10 stems each of blueberries and/or rose hips

FOLIAGE OF CHOICE: at least 10 stems each of hosta leaves, silver mound and/or plume poppy foliage

vase ½–¾ filled with lukewarm water and Chrysal or Floralife

florist's knife and/or scissors

newspaper or flower wrap

rubber band or clear hair tie

ribbon (optional)

create:

TECHNIQUE: the bouquet is built in your hands, with the aid of a tabletop

CONTAINER OF CHOICE: round clear glass vase, 5"–7" (13cm–18cm) high and 3"–5" (8cm–13cm) diameter

PHOTOS BY LISA GEORGE

master class

Arranging a bouquet in your hands—particularly determining the best grip with which to hold the flowers as you work—takes practice. You need to keep your fingers loose enough to move the flowers around and to avoid crunching them together, but tight enough to control their position.

Positioning the blooms takes careful consideration—you want to make sure all the flowers can be seen and are not hiding behind or underneath each other. Foliages that bend should be placed on the edges as they lend themselves to draping; those that are bolder and more upright should be arranged in the base. Think about how each of the foliages grow and arrange them in that way.

Likewise, remember to consider the vertical position of each component (some could be slightly raised or sunken to highlight a particular texture, shape or color) as well as its horizontal component. If you can master this technique, your hard work will be evident in the stunning results.

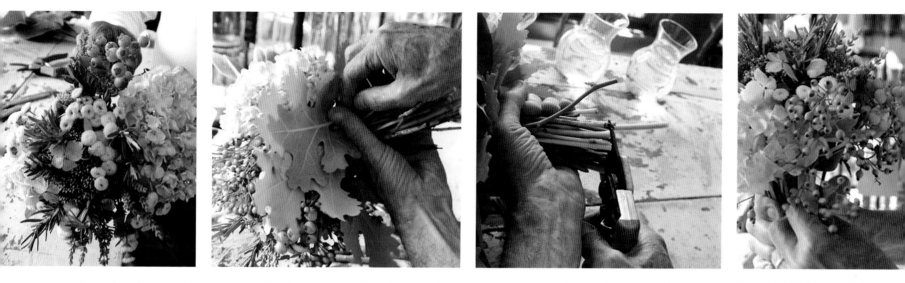

1. Gather the materials on your worktable so they are all within plain sight and easy reach. Review their shapes and textures, noting which can be used as flat and wide components of the bouquet, upright and straight, soft and wispy. Select a straight, hard stem to begin your bouquet. Here I began with rosemary.

2. Hold the first stem in your hand, and one at a time, add one or two stems of each component you have chosen for your bouquet, building your arrangement in one hand while adding stems with the other. I began by adding large, dominant flowers first (hydrangea or sedum) and then moving onto the smaller components.

3. Continue building your bouquet outward with additional elements, being careful to keep it balanced, creating symmetry within the arrangement. (Again, save the most delicate material for later.)

4. Work the arrangement in your hands to keep everything aligned, twisting your fingers and carefully interlocking the stems wherever necessary for them to hold their position. Cluster smaller delicate flowers and herbs together so they reflect their natural appearance and stand out as stronger components in the finished arrangement.

5. Save the most delicate or accent flowers for last to weave, or "sew," into the top center of the arrangement. Position them by loosening your grip on the arrangement, placing each stem carefully in the desired spot, pulling it through the bottom, and then tightening your grip.

6. After you are happy with the composition of your bouquet, add foliage as an outer trim. When selecting and positioning these stems, remember that firmer foliage can help floppier blooms stay in place.

7. Take a final look at the bouquet from all angles, inserting a few additional blossoms wherever necessary to perfectly balance the bouquet.

8. Trim the stems flush at the bottom of the bouquet to your desired length. Apply a rubber band to the stems. Either add a ribbon to create a handheld bouquet, or place the arrangement in a simple glass vase for display.

master class

Not all flowers have good posture. If a stem is too floppy or heavy to weave into the center of your bouquet, carefully arrange sturdier stems around it to help to hold it into position. You can also position curved stems in the opposite direction of their natural curve to make them stand up straight.

TROPICALS

A relatively recent green hybrid with a brushstroke of white variegation is gaining attention in the flower world. It's called the green goddess calla lily, and I arrange it more freely than white callas because it reminds me of foliages. Green goddess is long lasting, not cost prohibitive and available year-round—it might also surprise guests in the way that other unique, lesser known tropical flowers do.

Heliconia, for example, encompasses several types that resemble birds. There are others reminiscent of hanging claws, as red as cooked lobsters. Some even have yellow tips, and look a little like they could eat you. New hybrids of protea may remind you of a plant from another galaxy. To witness the opposite extreme, watch the delicate blooming of blushing bride. Of course, bird of paradise and anthurium are what most people know in this category, as well as an array of orchids, callas and leaves so big they might convince you to wallpaper one of your rooms in jungle prints!

From top: Heliconia, bird of paradise, green goddess calla lilies
GREEN GODDESS PHOTO BY CYNTHIA BLACK
Opposite page: Astilbe (far left) and "Blushing Bride" protea cut to various heights and arranged in clear, geometric glass vases
PHOTO BY BRIE WILLIAMS

NOTES ON SUMMER FLOWERS AND GRASSES

For a further look at arranging some of the most popular seasonal summer flowers, consider using Hybrid's arranging techniques with one or more of the following beautiful blooms.

Agapanthus

agapanthus: These flowers, which bloom in whites and deep blues, are best grown in Holland and California and range from three to six dollars a stem.

allium: Who knew onions could be so beautiful? Many Dutch and American varieties of this bloom are available in shades of purple and in sizes from petite to giant, ranging from three to ten dollars per stem. They're long lasting, but keep in mind that they smell like … onions.

alstroemeria: Also known as the Peruvian lily, alstroemeria comes in many colors and is best when imported from South America, Canada and California. Even for the best quality, you'll pay only between two and four dollars per stem.

astilbe: This delicate, fluffy and fragrant flower comes in pink and white and costs between three and five dollars per stem when bought locally during the summer season.

Allium

Astilbe PHOTO BY BRIE WILLIAMS

Alstroemeria PHOTO BY BRIE WILLIAMS

carnation: Although good-quality carnations are available year round at a good price, they are a great summer flower because they fit the season's laid-back mood and are durable in heat (and especially long lasting if kept in air conditioning).

cat tail foliage: These common plants (also known as "punks") come at a very low cost, but you can likely find and pick them yourself. I like the thinner ones: Keep them clean and put a drop of bleach in the water. Clean and arrange these stems graphically for a fabulous look.

chamomile: Opt for local or Dutch product when buying chamomile, which ranges between one and three dollars a stem and comes in white, yellow, green or a daisy type (pictured). This casual and unpretentious flower is great for adding life to your kitchen during the summer months.

cornflower: Many people don't know that this classic blue flower also comes in pink and white. Buy locally or Dutch-grown blooms, and expect to pay between five and ten dollars a bunch.

Carnations PHOTO BY BRIE WILLIAMS

Cornflowers

Chamomile

Cat tail foliage

dahlia: Growing in many colors, shapes and sizes, dahlia can be found in local abundance in season, costing only about one dollar per stem; imported blooms will cost twice as much.

daisy: Always inexpensive, always charming, most daisies are from California and cost between five and eight dollars per bunch. To help maintain your arrangement, add a drop of bleach to the water and be sure to keep it clean.

delphenium: This flower's colors range from deep purple to blue to pink and white. The larger varieties are among the most impressive tall flowers available. In the flower industry they are called "Dutch pride" because of their extraordinary beauty. At a wide range of three to twenty dollars per stem, shop for blooms grown in California, South America, Canada and Holland.

eremurus: This strong, tall and graphic bloom comes in shades of yellow, white and orange and is typically priced between three and ten dollars per stem. Buy it from the United States, Holland and Canada.

Dahlia

Daisies

Eremurus

Delphenium

126

euphorbia: This soft green foliage can be used on its own or as filler. Grow this in your own garden, or if you can't find it locally, buy bunches from South America or Holland at fifteen to twenty-five dollars per bunch or about two dollars per stem.

garden rose: The cashmere of the rose world, the garden rose blooms in endless colors and with a hefty price tag, at eight to twelve dollars per stem. The most popular are English garden rose varieties, the Austin rose being preeminent, though you can also find fragrant varieties from California that have an antique look.

gerbera daisy: These modern, graphic flowers, from three to six dollars each, are best grown in California, Canada and Israel.

herbs: Oregano, rosemary, mint, lavender, thyme, sage and other freshly grown herbs from supermarkets, roadside stands or cut from the garden can make wonderful arrangements. You'll find local product for about five dollars a bunch; imported from South America or Holland, bunches cost closer to fifteen dollars.

Euphorbia

Garden roses PHOTO BY LISA GEORGE

Gerbera daisies PHOTO BY BRIE WILLIAMS

Herbs PHOTO BY BRIE WILLIAMS

Hosta

Irises PHOTO BY LISA GEORGE

Lisianthus

hosta: These common garden plants grow easily locally, or purchase them from Holland. Either way, you'll pay between three and five dollars.

iris: At two to three dollars per stem, most irises available are grown in California.

lily: If you've had your fill of callas, try arranging some oriental lilies, best from Canada and Holland, at six to twelve dollars a stem.

lisianthus: Single and double flowers in many long-lasting colors, lisianthus love warm weather. Varieties are constantly being introduced, among them the new green double "mariachi." Buy American, Canadian, Dutch or Israeli product.

monkshood: Opt for South American and Dutch varieies of this tall, strong flower, priced between three and five dollars per stem.

Lilies PHOTO BY LISA GEORGE

Monkshood

Phlox

Snapdragons PHOTO BY LISA GEORGE

Solidagos PHOTO BY BRIE WILLIAMS

phlox: Buy this colorful bloom from Holland, California or Israel at three to five dollars per stem.

snapdragon: At two to three dollars, these stems are best locally or from Florida, California, Canada or South America.

solidago: This bloom is priced between one and two dollars per stem; buy local or South American varieties.

highlight: snapdragon

When florets are held back and squeezed, the mouth of a dragon will open; hence, the name of a classic bloom from the spring to fall gardens. Snapdragons, too beautiful for a "common" flower classification, beloved of all children (and a number of adults as well), allow height in an arrangement and lend themselves to tall graphic and vertical designs. Blooms come in a wide array of colors from purples to lavenders, yellows to oranges, and pinks to reds. Grow them in your own garden or buy them from a local greenhouse; Florida and California provide strong product and South American flowers are available year-round. Canadian snapdragons have a homegrown hewn, which is particularly attractive in comparison to the mass-produced look of so many flowers. Homespun florals remind us of other times— better times, perhaps. Pause with them for a moment of good cheer, whether you're under ten years old or over a hundred.

Steel grass PHOTO BY BRIE WILLIAMS

Summer grasses PHOTO BY LISA GEORGE

Summer hydrangea PHOTO BY LISA GEORGE

Sunflowers

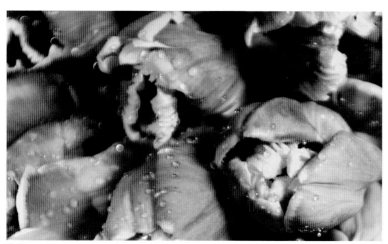

Tulips PHOTO BY BRIE WILLIAMS

steel grass: One of my favorites, and inexpensive—buy locally grown product.

summer grasses: Abundance is key in working with these grasses. Locally grown bunches range between two and six dollars.

summer hydrangea: Opt for American or Dutch blooms, ranging from four to twenty dollars per stem.

sunflower: In the summer, these wonderfully showy blooms are everywhere. Buy local stems at one to three dollars.

tulip: Buy product from Holland, ranging from two to three dollars per stem. Don't be afraid to experiment with the many varieties available, like the orange parrot tulips shown here.

A stunningly modern display of steel grass in a tall, graphic vase
PHOTO BY BRIE WILLIAMS

130

131

Orange parrot tulips displayed in a cheerful lime
green wooden cylinder

PHOTOS BY BRIE WILLIAMS

A bouquet of summer field flowers that combines white lilacs with purple vernonia, white wax flowers, blue gentian, white stock and purple lavender in a black wire basket covered with fresh moss

A sweet-smelling summer composition that mixes quinces and green viburnum berries with white hydrangea, white miniature calla lilies, white dahlias, white freesia, geranium foliage and yellow star of Bethlehem (also known as chincherinchee) in a white ceramic vase

PHOTOS BY BRIE WILLIAMS

chapter six

tre – autumn

NOVEMBER NOTEBOOK

Autumn often conjures images of a cornucopia rather than a flower bouquet. These months bring the festive, almost Tuscan abundance—*abbondanza*—of apples and pumpkins, nuts and mums, ruddy Bosc pears and purple plums in a bouquet of autumn colors. I find myself thinking of a warm, Italian twist on Thanksgiving: chrysanthemums, cock's combs, late snapdragons and indulging in a lot of anything. Among my favorite unexpected fall blooms are vibernum in dark tones, carnations from Italy and locally grown fall pods and grasses. We blanket our wooden dining table with rich linens and down the center arrange a garland of flowers and leaves. For florals, choose vases of family significance—they don't have to match—or simple glass containers with four- to five-inch (ten- to thirteen-centimeter) openings. The seasonal arrangements should be spaced equally down the table runner. Between them,

tuck in ornamentals (try votives, miniature pumpkins, novel gourds or Granny Smith apples). Rediscover your favorite autumn blooms by the light of some festive candles. When you blow them out, make a wish.

A richly varied composition consisting of speckled cream and pink hydrangea, double tulips, dark pink mini callas, helleborus, concord grapes, plums and blackberries in a pewter bowl
PHOTOS BY BRIE WILLIAMS

AUTUMN HUES

The lazy summer bouquets, loose and carefree, are gone now. Leaves rattle on the walk. Black and orange Chinese lanterns in carved-out pumpkins are outside for Halloween. Mums, in both familiar and novel varieties, such as "Santini" (interesting, small scale and beautiful), celebrate Thanksgiving. Fall's garden, hardy and muted, is proudly unsophisticated, with only sparse, steadfast survivors. The exotic grande dames, their luxury, their sensuality, are last season's memory. All of my experience told me to use what was outside my window, despite the lack of fresh growth. Then, working intuitively and relying on imports, I decided it was time to break even the time-honored rules and experiment with some nontraditional bouquets.

Each fall, I look for the dominant hue in the turning foliage to inspire my arrangements. This year it's neon orange. Throughout this chapter you'll see bright, bold gerbera daisies, electric femma roses and hypernicum berries. But these quick and easy arrangements of orange "Sandersonia" Chinese lanterns (opposite page) and sweet peas (at left) are two of my favorites. By now, my Hybrid Tabletop and Hybrid Matrix techniques will seem very familiar to you. Next year, the autumn color will be yours to choose.

Above: An abundance of sweet peas in seasonal colors, their stems carefully interwoven PHOTO BY CYNTHIA FERNALD
Opposite page: "Sandersonia" Chinese lanterns arranged with the Hybrid Matrix Technique in a glass vase PHOTO BY BRIE WILLIAMS

When used correctly, even a spring bloom can scream "fall baroque." Sometimes it's best to use flowers in an unexpected, chic, subtle way, just as a fashion designer puts a twist on a basic dress. Flowers are, after all, an architectural variety of shapes and colors—and similar to clothing (which also becomes more sophisticated in the fall). These orange tulips—like sweet peas and miniature calla lilies—are irresistable imports from below the equator during the autumn months.

Parrot tulips in a tall, rectangular green ceramic vase

Peonies from New Zealand and Chile take us from shades of orange to heavenly salmon. These varieties, named "Coral Charm" and "Coral Sunset," will stun guests in glass or antique bronze containers. Place them at equal height and space them as evenly as possible. Peonies are easy to work with—the truth is, once they start opening, they'll arrange themselves.

Above: A beautiful "Coral Sunset" peony
Opposite page: New Zealand "Coral Charm" peonies in a striking footed vase PHOTO BY BRIE WILLIAMS

hybrid flowers and fruit in floral foam

You might liken the technique used to create this deceptively simple but bountiful arrangement—built in OASIS Floral Foam—to weaving fabric. It combines seasonal blooms with fruit (not too ripe) of colors that match the chosen flowers as closely as possible. The design is then complemented with foliage, colorful berries and delicate, clustered flowers.

prepare:

12–20 each of seasonal fruit (I chose apples and pears), hydrangea, geranium foliage, andromeda and roses

floral sticks or skewers

florist's knife

OASIS Floral Foam

watering can filled with water and Chrysal or Floralife

create:

TECHNIQUE: build arrangment in OASIS Floral Foam

CONTAINER OF CHOICE: rustic flowerpot or pail

master class

There are several kinds of OASIS Floral Foam. The standard variety, which is used for this arrangement, has a medium density that works well to secure woody, medium-weight stems. If you are working with particularly delicate or extra-heavy stems, you may find that another variety works best for your needs. Be sure to look at all the available options and follow the manufacturer's instructions for preparing the foam for use.

When working with any type of floral foam, be sure to anchor all the stems deep into the foam so they'll be able to hydrate. Always add water daily.

PHOTOS BY LISA GEORGE

1 Use your florist's knife to cut a block of OASIS Floral Foam to the size and shape of your container. You'll want it to fit snugly so the arrangement does not shift (especially if you'll be using heavy stems). Here I've elected to use a watertight container placed inside a decorative rustic pail as the basis of my arrangment. First, measure or (if you're brave) eyeball the size of a block that would fit snugly in the center. Cut the block to size.

2 If your container is round, use your knife to shave the foam block's corners until they will better conform to the circular shape.

3 Place the foam in your container. If it does not fit inside, use your florist's knife to make any necessary adjustments. If you are working with a square container, you are ready for step 5.

4 If you are working with a round container, cut a few more strips of foam to fill any gaps around the edges. Slip these pieces snugly inside until the majority of the interior of your container is filled with foam.

5 Using your watering can, pour water over the foam until it is soaking wet.

6 Begin with one of the largest or most abundant materials you plan to use in your arrangement—here I'm starting with some hydrangea. Push a single stem firmly and deeply into the center of the foam to create your starting point and to establish the height of your arrangement.

7 Go on to add another stem of the same bloom (again, hydrangea here) close to the first stem but at a different height and angle.

8 Continue to add other full blooms and clusters of smaller stems, slowly building a somewhat triangular shape as the start of your arrangement. Creating this structure now will help the finished composition look more natural.

master class

While working, save beautiful buds
and side shoots from your flowers.
You can use them to add a desirable
custom organic quality to your
other compositions.

9 Continue adding other elements of your composition—geranium, andromeda—to transform your preliminary triangle into a loose, symmetrical shape. Aim to evenly distribute each type of stem in small clusters to create a look that is natural, not polka dotted. Take your time as you work, and experiment until you get the feel for working with this type of composition.

10 When your composition is full and even, begin to add the fruit. Spear each piece firmly with a pair of skewers or floral sticks (using two helps keep them secure, but it's also best if the fruit is firm, not too ripe).

Spear any side of the fruit that is bruised or blemished so you can hide unattractive parts inside the arrangement or, when working with pears, skewer the bottoms so you can arrange them stem-side-up. Begin adding the fruit in clusters of two or three, spacing it evenly throughout the arrangement. Check for any holes in your composition and fill them with fruit or additional stems as a final, finishing touch.

master class

For a centerpiece, keep the height at or below 12" (30cm) so as not to obstruct the sight line across the table. But the flowers themselves do not all have to be the same height—small variation will create depth and texture, and the overall feel will be cohesive.

AUTUMN OASIS

Once you master the technique of working with OASIS Floral Foam, you can add a new dimension to your repertoire of arrangements. To start on your own, try your hand at a single-stem arrangement. This simple seasonal cluster of hypernicum berries, arranged in OASIS Floral Foam, can last a month and is versatile in its use—consider placing it low, on a coffee table, for example.

Hypernicum berries, shown at left paired with an arrangement of dogwood branches and curly willow branches, and shown in more detail on the opposite page

PHOTOS BY BRIE WILLIAMS

To create multiflower arrangements that evoke a rich baroque feeling perfect for the crisp fall months, cluster flowers of each type throughout a composition to make a stronger impression across a room. (Neglecting to cluster the flowers properly, however, will create a polka-dotted effect.) Hydrangeas are a good base for floral compositions—in autumn, you can fill in the natural openings with anything from chocolate cosmos to black seed pods, from roses and "Blushing Bride" protea. Find a container you've never used and show it off.

A fall composition of pink and green hydrangea, chocolate cosmos and black pepperberry in florist's foam

PHOTOS BY BRIE WILLIAMS

Speckled cream and pink hydrangea, double purple tulips, dark pink
mini callas, helleborus, concord grapes, plums and blackberries in a
pewter bowl

PHOTOS BY BRIE WILLIAMS

An orange monochromatic composition that combines femma roses,
ranunculus, orange chincherinchee, hypernicum berries, three different
types of geranium foliage, red rose hips, Mandarin oranges and
nectarines in an antique copper bucket

PHOTOS BY BRIE WILLIAMS

NOTES ON FALL FLOWERS AND FOLIAGES:

For more innovative autumn arrangements in rich seasonal hues,
try Hybrid's arranging techniques with one or more of the following.

amaranthus: This tall, exotic garden flower blooms in the late summer and fall in many varieties, such as the brilliant orange "Forest Fire" shown here. One hanging variety, "Love Lies Bleeding," looks as if it has burgundy dreadlocks; others are green or speckled. Buy local (one dollar each) or imported (two dollars each) stems.

bittersweet vine: These understated orange and yellow vines swirl and twist themselves beautifully into natural arrangements. These come in bunches of ten, ranging in price from five (at farmer's markets) to twenty dollars.

celosia (cock's comb): Seasonal varieties bloom in an array of feathery plumes in fall colors, some of which have a wonderful velvet-like texture. Arrange them in a composition or as a dome. Buy them locally grown for a dollar per stem, or opt for European varieties at three to six dollars per stem.

Amaranthus

Bittersweet vines

Celosia (cock's comb)

Chinese lanterns PHOTO BY BRIE WILLIAMS

Chrysanthemums PHOTO BY BRIE WILLIAMS

chinese lantern: Ranging from orange and whimsical to deep black, these blooms can be either imported or locally grown. Arrange them by themselves, without other flowers. Many varieties are good for drying, as they maintain their color. They can be pricey at three dollars per stem.

chrysanthemum: All things have their season and fall belongs to mums. Very long lasting and available in endless varieties and colors, the flower is sometimes underappreciated. Buy local or imported and arrange in abundance; expect to pay about one dollar per stem.

crabapple: Purchase crabapple in bunches. Arrange it alone or with other fall foliages (such as viburnum and maple) in a tall 12"–18" (30cm–46cm) vase with a 5"–8" (13cm–20cm) opening, or add it to a rich composition. Buy these branches freshly culled from trees, locally at about fifteen dollars for five stems. If you buy them imported, be prepared to pay up to seventy-five dollars for the same quantity.

Crabapples PHOTO BY LISA GEORGE

Dianthus PHOTO BY BRIE WILLIAMS   Hydrangea PHOTO BY BRIE WILLIAMS   Kale

dianthus: The carnation has been hybridized to create this beautiful butterfly. Opt for Dutch product at three to four dollars per stem.

hydrangea: Newer varieties have been hybridized to create a great range of fall colors, some blended in fascinating combinations. Buy locally or imported stems ranging from two to twenty dollars each.

kale: This cabbage, available in green, white or purple, can be used to achieve a strong architectural look in an arrangement. You can buy both local and imported varieties at three to six dollars a stem.

maple: Buy this autumn foliage locally in bunches to add a classic look to any seasonal arrangement. It comes freshly culled from trees in big bunches for ten to twenty dollars.

pear foliage: Buy big, locally grown bunches of this shiny, strong foliage freshly culled from trees. Expect to pay between ten and twenty dollars.

Maple

Pear foliage

Sedum

Seedpods

sedum: These heavy-stemmed beauties are long lasting. The "Autumn Joy" variety—green when undeveloped, then turning pink or red—is my favorite. You'll find them locally grown for two to six dollars a stem.

seedpod: Look in the garden to see what has gone to seed. Then use the pods to make a bouquet exotic and unusual. Beyond locally grown varieties, you'll find many imported seedpods to choose from. Buy them in fifteen-dollar bunches.

sunflower: Don't miss the brown and variegated fall tones, available at three to five dollars per stem.

vibernum: Arrange vibernum in floral compositions, alone or with other fall foliage. Cut the stems to length and arrange them in water so they are spaced apart, with visible branch lines. The end result should appear graceful, like a well-manicured shrub or tree. Vibernum are culled from bushes, and you can expect to pay fifty dollars for a group of five six-foot-tall (two-meter-tall) stems that are locally grown; less readily available stems could cost up to seventy-five dollars.

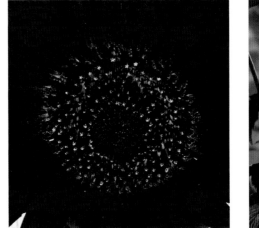

Sunflower

Vibernum

Above: A charming, understated way to display this favorite fall
composition of mine; Opposite page: Neon pink tropical butterfly
dianthus PHOTOS BY BRIE WILLIAMS

Gerbera daisies in a brilliant, almost neon orange, arranged using
the Hybrid Tabletop Technique

PHOTOS BY BRIE WILLIAMS

An elegant seasonal showcase of orange parrot tulips alongside gypsy curiosa roses, green snowball viburnum, protea, kangaroo paw and geranium foliage in a mossy terra-cotta compote

chapter seven

quattro – winter

DECEMBER NOTEBOOK

Winter taps into the senses with pine, spruce and cedar. Shades of green turn to blue, and eventually fade to gray. As we get closer to the holidays, splashes of winterberry brighten the darkening evenings. Red flowers are most popular this time of year, but I also favor winter white— silvery blue candlelight gives them a cool glow. We start decorating on the first of December, both at Hybrid and at home. Inside and out, my house will be boughed, garlanded and wreathed with lasting seasonal foliages. Without the trimmings of bulbs, balls and bows, I'll keep the exterior arrangements in place through February; it adds a bit of décor in the absence of our outdoor plantings. Last year, I left a pair of magnificent magnolia wreaths on the front windows until April 1. I just didn't want to take them down.

Paperwhites and cedar centerpiece

PHOTO BY BRIE WILLIAMS

WHITES OF WINTER

As you decorate with flowers for the coldest season, opt for practical, long-lasting blooms. Mums in varieties like "Snowdrift," "Spider" and "Statesman" are a beautiful winter white and will last a minimum of two weeks. Old-fashioned large white "Football" mums, often referred to as "Deco," are among my seasonal favorites. You might also select simple arrangements of carnations. Baby's breath is another long-time favorite of mine—and it's quite the rage right now. Tuck it into your Christmas tree, create a garland by weaving it through evergreen foliage or even leave it by itself in dazzling mass abundance. In January, as winter hits its true peak, visit greenhouses for flowering branches, as well as bulb plants like the paperwhite, amaryllis, hyacinth, tulip and muscari. You'll see many of these showcased in signature arrangements throughout this chapter. Let them inspire you to build your own creations.

From top: Spider mum, statesman mums, snowdrift mums
Opposite page: Old-fashioned large white "Football," or "Deco,"
mums in rectangular stone vases PHOTO BY BRIE WILLIAMS

CHRISTMAS

Think evergreens, poinsettias and other red flowers. For a modern approach to an old tradition, choose poinsettias in the newer varieties of white, rose or salmon pink. (If you have a pet, though, beware that these plants are poisonous.)

HANUKKAH

Place white tulips in a cobalt blue vase. Or arrange seasonal greenery with berries, fruit and nuts. For a brighter, more contemporary approach, add a few of your favorite white blooms to festive silver foliage.

NEW YEAR'S DAY

Choose any flower you like, but make its color white—it signifies a fresh start.

ST. VALENTINE'S DAY

Roses are the tried-and-true favorites. But watch out for holiday price mark-ups. Since February is also the beginning of spring bulb season, you might try other red flowers, such as tulips. They'll be less typical than roses (which might

Poinsettia

Rose

not be at their best quality in times of high demand), but don't worry—they'll still dazzle.

ST. PATRICK'S DAY

Shamrocks, of course! Try this: Carve the center portion out of a flat, long baking potato. Place potted clover (about two inches, or five centimeters) right in the spud: Instant Irish. Don't forget to plant the potato outside when the holiday is over—and don't be surprised if you decide to make this innovative luck-of-the-Irish display again next year.

Shamrocks

Opposite: A graphic arrangement of white tulips in a white ceramic bowl, perfect for celebrating winter while anticipating the arrival of spring
PHOTO BY BRIE WILLIAMS

cedar and white centerpiece

We've always been taught to use our imaginations at Christmas. How perfect then that this simple holiday arrangement conjures visions of snowfall in forests. If you'd like, you can substitute holly, juniper or pine foliage for the cedar base. While cedar and other evergreens will last weeks, you'll need to replace the flowers after they're spent. In lieu of paperwhites (shown here), you might substitute chamomile blooms (shown on the following pages) or even pompoms, carnations, miniature carnations, gerbera daisies, tulips, roses, miniature calla lilies or anemones.

prepare:

25–50 paperwhites (shown here) or chamomile (shown on the following pages)

3 handfuls (about 20 stems) cedar twigs

watering can filled with lukewarm water and Chrysal or Floralife

florist's knife and/or scissors

OASIS Floral Foam cut to fit your container of choice (as shown on page 148)

create:

TECHNIQUE: build arrangement in OASIS Floral Foam (see page 146 for detailed instructions, and pages 178–179 for a visual how-to on this arrangement)

CONTAINER OF CHOICE: ceramic oval with a matte white finish

master class

There are times when the shape of the vase you've chosen will help you determine how you want to shape your arrangement. When constructing a centerpiece like this, be sure to keep its container in mind from start to finish.

1 Place your floral foam, cut to size with your florist's knife, inside your container of choice. Add water to the foam until it's soaking wet. Wipe any excess from your vase.

2 With a composition of this nature, you will build the base of foliage first, then add flowers last. Begin by selecting a strong cedar stem and inserting it deeply into one side of the foam. This will establish the width of your arrangement.

3 Continue adding one strong cedar stem to each of the remaining three sides of the foam, establishing a circumference for your composition.

4 Insert a sprig of cedar into the top center of the arrangement, being careful to choose a stem that will properly establish a good height for the arrangement.

5 Continue adding cedar until you've created a full, dome-shaped arrangement using your initial branches as a guide. Work until you're happy with the shape and fullness of the arrangement, and the foam is completely hidden.

6 Take a paperwhite (shown on the previous pages) or chamomile (shown here) stem, trim it to the appropriate length for your composition and carefully push it into the foam, taking care that it neither becomes hidden by the foliage nor protrudes from the arrangement too far.

7 Continue adding flowers until they are evenly spaced throughout the composition, adding just the right amount of white.

When combining seasonal colors, try using the same flower type in different colors, and keep the presentation graphic. It will make preparations easier and simpler, especially during hectic preparations for holiday guests.

The signature Hybrid twist on festive red and white tulips

PHOTOS BY BRIE WILLIAMS

SIMPLY FLOWERS

Of course, there are reasons (if you need a reason at all) to arrange flowers during the winter months beyond holiday settings. In fact, some flowers aren't seen at this time of year solely because of traditional floral expectations, not because of lack of availability or affordability. Whether we use them or not (and we should), I would be remiss not to mention my favorite high-quality blooms that are so easily attained and yet so seldom used during the winter months.

French anemones are available in several colors, but my favorites come in white with black centers and a soft blush running through them. Arrange them using the Hybrid Tabletop Technique. All at once, they manage to be bold as well as delicate—an elegant combination.

Anemones arranged simply in a crystal vase with a signature twist
PHOTOS BY BRIE WILLIAMS

182

Winter begins the season for tall and sinewy French tulips. Handling these flowers with care is key to arranging them successfully. When you first receive them, remove the bottom foliage. (The flowers usually come with quite a bit of composted soil; gently shave what cannot be easily pulled off.) Rinse and refrigerate them in deep water—this will stiffen the stems, which may be a bit limp at the start. Arrange them using the Hybrid Matrix Technique, shaping the flowers by hand as needed (work carefully—they'll easily snap).

Decadent French tulips in a lovely winter white
PHOTO BY BRIE WILLIAMS

Ranunculus come from France, Italy, Holland and New Zealand in the winter (and grow in the United States during the summer months). In recent years the little cabbage rose floret has been hybridized into many new and beautiful varieties, from piccolo to giganteum in size, with a wide spectrum of colors. Arrange large quantities with the Hybrid Tabletop Technique for a stunning effect.

A dome of deep red Italian ranunculus in a wide, low glass vase
PHOTO BY BRIE WILLIAMS

Opposites attract, and the aesthetic contradiction of winter and tropical exotics can be stunning, as evidenced by the widespread popularity of orchids during this season. They are long lasting and easy to work with; bring a potted orchid indoors in winter for a chance to watch nature in action as the plant develops out and curls in to seed. Be careful when placing orchids on heaters and near fireplaces, though—they hate dry heat. At the opposite extreme, windowsills and winter drafts may prove too cold for them. Lots of humidity and good indirect light are best. Other tropical exotics to include early in the new year include stephanotis, gardenias, Eucharist lilies, Nerine lilies and jasmine.

A winter arrangement of jasmine and silver foliage
PHOTOS BY BRIE WILLIAMS

green dendrobium orchids

One of the least expensive varieties of orchids, dendrobiums are certainly not one of the least beautiful. These monochromatic blooms bring a breath of fresh air to any room in the winter months. Before you begin your arrangement, decide whether or not you'd like the bouquet to be viewed from all sides (as the one shown here can be) or positioned against a background, as on a mantel. Deciding where you want to put the arrangement first will help you determine the best way to distribute your stems in your container of choice using the tried-and-true Hybrid Matrix Technique.

prepare:

35 dendrobium orchid stems

vase filled with lukewarm water and Chyrsal or Floralife

florist's knife and/or scissors

create:

TECHNIQUE: Hybrid Matrix

CONTAINER OF CHOICE: 6" × 9" (15cm × 23cm) traditional glass vase

master class

Follow all of the standard Hybrid Matrix Technique steps to arrange these stems—as described in chapter three and as shown here—distributing them evenly and systematically as you work. These orchid stems will stay where you put them. If they are not forming the exact lines you are hoping for, don't struggle to force them into something they're not. The imperfections are natural and simple.

There was a time when orchids were the dominant species on the planet because of their ability to procreate independently. Today, 18"–20" (46cm–51cm) tall, long-lasting and simple, phalaenopsis orchids are the epitome of contemporary style in florals. They're dragons who smile, as frightening as any flower would ever dare become. The ancient Greeks found the attractive petal formations "moth-like," which gives us the first part of the name.

The flowers themselves actually evolved to look like insects in their successful bid to attract them. Following the flower's fragrance, a bee, wasp or other insect comes to the orchid's throat and becomes enmeshed in nectar. Its only chance for escape is to climb up and around the lip. Whether or not the insect knows fertilization of an egg is taking place by sloshing through the separated sexual parts of the plant is not known, and it probably doesn't matter. It simply flies off. The orchid knows, however. Within twenty-four hours, the floret folds up and falls to the ground, beginning a new life cycle.

Unlike the beautiful, if old-fashioned, cattleya—so prominent in mid-twentieth-century American culture for proms and Mother's Day—phalaenopsis orchids are on a new trajectory to corporate board rooms and homes as startling objects of graphic beauty. A New York Fashion Week re-invigorated the family during the mid-'90s, when fuchsia Phalaenopsis orchids were given to out-of-town journalists, causing an explosion of fascination. For those mourning the passing of Technicolor slow dances and orchid corsages in plastic boxes, there's even been a renewed interest in the flowers at proms. Today, reinvented and worthy of Cleopatra, the florets are seen wrapped around and up the arm, wired, slinking and sexy.

NOTES ON WINTER FLOWERS, FOLIAGE AND BRANCHES

Chase away the midwinter blahs with arrangements of these wonderful seasonal blooms, stems and clippings.

Amaryllis PHOTO BY BRIE WILLIAMS

Anemones PHOTO BY BRIE WILLIAMS

amaryllis: Buy amaryllis from the United States, Holland, France and Canada. Locally grown extra-fancy-grade product can cost twelve dollars per stem. Amaryllis should have three to four blooms per head; a two-bloom stem would be ten dollars or less.

anemone: You can buy anemones in the winter from local greenhouses, or opt for imported French or Dutch product. These blooms average three dollars per stem.

baby's breath: At fifteen dollars for a market bunch, the best baby's breath grows in South and Central America.

Baby's breath

Gardenia floret

Jasmine florets

Stephanotis florets

florets: Buy florets—try gardenias, jasmine and stephanotis, to name a few favorites—that come from California. None are cost-prohibitive, but these very fragrant blooms are mostly used in wired work (stephanotis is a traditional bridal bloom) or as floating flowers.

french tulip: Opt for product from France or California at six to eight dollars per stem for the best grade.

French tulips PHOTO BY BRIE WILLIAMS

195

Hybrid nerine lilies PHOTO BY BRIE WILLIAMS

hybrid nerine lily: Among my favorites blooms, Nerine
lilies are available from New Zealand and Holland and priced
at five to ten dollars per stem, depending on type and quality.

Italian ranunculus PHOTO BY BRIE WILLIAMS

Orchids

Paperwhites PHOTO BY BRIE WILLIAMS

Privet branches PHOTO BY BRIE WILLIAMS

italian ranunculus: Small, delicate and unusual at three dollars per stem, these blooms should, of course, be imported from Italy.

orchid: The best blooms can be Dutch, Thai, Hawaiian or, yes, even local. Prices range from two dollars (dendrobium) to fifty dollars (for an extra-fancy cattleya). Most orchids are very long lasting.

paperwhite: Purchase paperwhites from local greenhouses or imported from Holland or New Zealand. On average, they're priced at one dollar per stem. They're available in many varieties, but be careful when deciding where to place an arrangement: They tend to smell unpleasant when fully developed, and the odor can be too much for certain areas of the home.

privet branch: These tall and clumsy branches can be used to create simple and elegant arrangements if you learn to work with them properly. Calculate your open space and be careful not to overfill the vase; you want the elegant natural lines of the wood to be seen. Buy locally culled stems in bunches of ten for twenty dollars; be prepared to pay thirty-five dollars for imported bunches.

quince branch: These are a favorite in our house. After the third frost, the buds are set in the white branches, and we bring them into our greenhouse to bloom. From bud to finish, they'll last three weeks. Purchase only locally grown quince branches; expect to pay $125 for enough to fill a substantially large vase.

winter foliage: Choose juniper, cedar, lamb's ear, silver mound—anything in silvers—eucalyptus or silver geranium foliage (which looks good in composition or by itself). Buy winter foliage locally; it's inexpensive and long lasting.

Quince branch

Lamb's ear

Eucalyptus

Opposite page: Seasonal favorites of mine, privet branches, displayed in a silver vase to achieve unexpected sophistication

PHOTO BY BRIE WILLIAMS

198

Above: Green dendrobium orchids in an understated glass vase—a hint of
the tropics during the winter months PHOTO BY BRIE WILLIAMS
Opposite: French tulips can add impressive height to any room in a tall
crystal vase PHOTO BY BRIE WILLIAMS

Anemones displayed in a crystal vase to show off their unique winter
blooms—like snowflakes, no two are alike

PHOTOS BY BRIE WILLIAMS

index